5.95

D1200953

THESE ARE THE
GREAT LAKES

Books by Phil Ault

THESE ARE THE GREAT LAKES

THIS IS THE DESERT

WONDERS OF THE MOSQUITO WORLD

THESE ARE THE GREAT LAKES

Phil Ault

ILLUSTRATED WITH PHOTOGRAPHS AND A MAP

DODD, MEAD & COMPANY
New York

FOR LINKEN

who finds the Great Lakes
as fascinating as the fjords

Contents

I

Meet the Five Sisters

The white man and the seven Indians had been paddling rhythmically for several hours, pushing their birch bark canoe through the sea. Jean Nicolet, ragged in the frontier garments he had worn for so many weeks, paused to look around him. He and his Huron companions were alone on the huge expanse of water, headed for the lowering sun.

A thousand miles back to the east, a dot in the wilderness, lay his home in the New World, Quebec. And three thousand miles beyond Quebec across the Atlantic Ocean, as though in a different world, was his native France. The year was 1634.

What was ahead? Only water for the moment. But Nicolet had been told of light- and smooth-skinned men living on the far edge of the sea. Surely these must be the inhabitants of China, the fabled land that the learned men of his day knew lay on the opposite side of the world from France. Now he, Jean Nicolet, *voyageur* and agent of the great Samuel de Champlain, was about to cross the western sea and reach the Orient.

Small pleasure craft now dot the Great Lakes where Indian canoes once glided.

Hour after hour the eight men paddled on through the gentle waves lapping around their craft. The blue-gray sea was capable of being tossed into tumultuous storms, but, as though extending a gentle welcome to the first white man to cross its waters, today it was calm and smiling.

They entered a channel leading into a long, narrowing bay. Believing his meeting with the Chinese at hand, Nicolet drew from his pack in the bottom of the canoe the ceremonial attire he had carried from Quebec for this moment—an Oriental damask robe decorated with flowers and colored birds. He slipped the robe over his rough clothing and, taking a pistol in each hand, stepped ashore to greet the assembled men, women, and children. Ceremoniously, he fired the pistols into the air.

Terror seized the women and children. They fled, frightened by the pale-skinned man who carried thunder in his hands. For Nicolet the meeting was even more disturbing. The people who welcomed him proved to be not Chinese but Winnebago Indians. This was not the shore of Cathay; it was the shore of Wisconsin on the Door Peninsula near the head of Green Bay. The western sea he had crossed was Lake Michigan.

Nicolet's mistake is not surprising when we realize how skimpy the knowledge of geography was 350 years ago. Men knew that the world was round but had little concept of how big it was. Everything on the western side of the Atlantic was almost unknown territory full of mystery and promise. There were no maps of the American mainland, and to a traveler who had been moving slowly westward for weeks in a canoe, Lake Michigan seemed both large enough and distant enough to be the rumored western sea.

Despite his disappointment, Nicolet has gone into history as the first white man to see Lake Michigan, one of the band of French explorers who revealed to seventeenth-century European civilization the existence of nature's spectacular phenomenon, the five Great Lakes. Until the Frenchmen came, the lakes had stood in forested isolation for untold years, seen only by a few Indians who camped on their shores.

Wild animals still populate forested areas in the remote regions of the Great Lakes. A bull moose at a salt lick is caught by a photographer on St. Ignace Island in Lake Superior.

Even in this day of supersonic speed, the size of the Great Lakes is impressive, forming as they do the largest reservoir of fresh water in the world. There are lonely places along their shores that are virtually unchanged since the explorers came. Elsewhere on the lake edges are mammoth cities of a size that would leave the explorers gasping in unbelief. Had someone with a vision of the future pointed his hand toward the southern end of Lake Michigan, where Chicago stands, and told Nicolet, "One day there will be buildings one hundred stories high," the Frenchman would have exclaimed, *"Mon Dieu!"* and thought the man crazy.

Sister ships in the C & O Railway trainferry fleet, S.S. *Badger* and S.S. *Spartan*, docked together at Ludington, Michigan.

Loading freight cars aboard the trainferry S.S. *Spartan* at Ludington, Michigan, for a trip across Lake Michigan to Wisconson. Staterooms, a dining room, and deck chairs provide passengers with a mini-cruise.

A traveler crossing Lake Michigan today along a route roughly parallel to Nicolet's but farther to the south sees things much differently than he did. Instead of a frail canoe, his vessel is a steel boat with an icebreaker prow, larger than some cargo ships on the oceans. The expanse of blue water and sky appears much as it did to the explorer. The difference is what man has done on the water and around it.

With a deep blast of its whistle, the boat slips away from its dock at Ludington, on the state of Michigan's western shore, and out into the lake. In its hold it carries twenty-eight railroad cars. Packed around them, and on the deck above, are nearly fifty automobiles and trailers. Hundreds of passengers line the rails or sit in the lounge and staterooms as the boat sails rapidly and smoothly southwestward toward Milwaukee on the Wisconsin side. A radar screen above the bridge revolves slowly, watching traffic on the lake. This is a Chesapeake and Ohio railroad ferry, one of a fleet that makes the ninety-mile journey daily, in winter when ice clogs the lake as well as in midsummer, when the tourists come.

As the sand dunes of the Michigan shore dwindle astern, a dark blob appears off the port bow. It grows and takes on the shape of a ship. Soon it passes on the left, a low, 700-foot-long vessel with superstructures at bow and stern separated by hundreds of feet of cargo space. This is a lake bulk carrier sailing north, empty, toward the Minnesota iron mines, after delivering its cargo of ore to the steel mills of Gary, Indiana. Thirty-thousand feet above, the sky is streaked by the jet trail of an airliner flying north from Chicago. No land can be seen. A young woman passenger, sunning herself on deck in a bathing suit, says to her friend, "This is almost like being on a Caribbean cruise."

Another ship crosses the ferry's bow, a cement-carrying vessel on her regular run between lake ports. And then another, different this time. The tall masts and cargo booms are the tipoff: it is a "salty." Flying the flag of Norway at her stern, the ocean freighter has brought a cargo of merchandise from Europe up the St. Lawrence River, through the locks of the St. Lawrence

The Sleeping Bear Dunes, the world's largest moving sand dunes, are a favorite place for photographers. They are on the Lake Michigan shoreline of West Michigan.

The trainferry S.S. *Spartan*, carrying railroad cars and automobiles, crossing Lake Michigan from Ludington, Michigan, to Milwaukee, Wisconsin. Passengers enjoy the relaxation of the trip, which takes about six hours.

Seaway, and the length of the Great Lakes to Milwaukee. As the ferry nears the Milwaukee breakwater, dozens of white sails billow and dip in the breeze like moths. Weekend sailors racing their private boats are making the turn around a buoy just outside the shipping lane.

The Great Lakes are many things—the makers of weather, the home of intricate fish life, a source of scenery and recreation for millions of persons, the creators of electric power, the scene of astounding feats of endurance by the explorers and of battles that shaped the future of North America, a sickening example of senseless pollution. Most of all, they are a highway of deep blue water that carries ships nearly halfway across the North American continent from the Atlantic Ocean toward the Pacific shore. And across these waters the products of the Midwestern heart of the United States and Canada are borne to ports throughout the world.

Often they are called the Five Sisters—Lakes Superior, Michigan, Huron, Erie, and Ontario. They hang like a cluster of

Lorado Taft's sculpture, "Fountain of the Great Lakes," popularly
called "The Five Sisters," at the Art Institute of Chicago

grapes on the map, surrounded for the most part by prairies and
remnants of the almost endless forest that covered the region
before the white men came to chop it down. Together they hold
half of the fresh water in the world.

Like five sisters in a family they have much in common, but
each has special characteristics. Through the middle of four of
them, all except Lake Michigan, the friendly border between the
United States and Canada runs for hundreds of miles.

A fountain of bronze by the eminent sculptor Lorado Taft,
called "Fountain of the Great Lakes," at the Art Institute in
Chicago depicts the Five Sisters in dramatic form. Standing at the
top of the group in flowing gown is a figure whose upraised
hands tilt a basin of water from which a splashing stream falls
into a basin held by two similarly garbed figures. The one at the
top represents Lake Superior, biggest, deepest, most primitive,
and farthest west of the five lakes, also the one at the highest

8

altitude, 600 feet above sea level. Superior is 350 miles long, 160 miles wide, and 1,333 feet deep at its maximum point. This makes it the largest fresh-water lake in the world. Only the salty Caspian Sea is a larger lake.

The two sisters below, catching Superior's waters in a common basin, are Lakes Michigan and Huron. They are depicted so because they are at the same sea level, linked by the Straits of Mackinac. Superior's waters drain into Huron, a drop of twenty-one feet, through the rapids of the St. Marys River at Sault Ste. Marie, site of the Soo Locks by which ships can bypass the rapids and travel between the lakes. Situated entirely within the United States, Lake Michigan, 345 miles long and 118 miles wide at its broadest, points south to Chicago. The shorter Lake Huron points south toward Detroit, 206 miles long and 101 miles wide. Michigan is deeper, 923 feet at maximum to Huron's 752 feet.

In the statuary group, the fountain's stream drops next into a

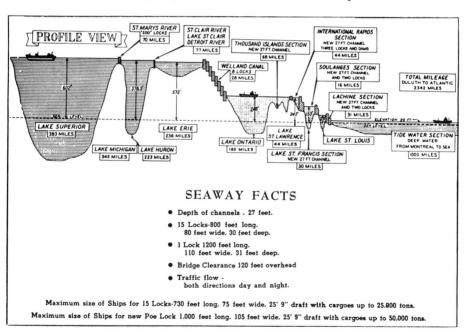

Profile view of Great Lakes

9

basin held by a sister who leans down, holding the vessel knee high. She represents Lake Erie, which lies in an east-west direction from Detroit on the west to Buffalo, New York, on the east. Erie is the next-to-smallest of the Great Lakes, 241 miles long and only 57 miles wide; also, it is the shallowest, 210 feet deep at maximum. Because of its relatively small volume of water and the large industrial cities that line its shores, Lake Erie has become the much-cited horrible example of water pollution, leading some conservationists to make the exaggerated statement that "Lake Erie is dead."

The water level in Erie is eight feet below that of Huron and Michigan, a gradual drop through the seventy-seven mile strait that is formed by the St. Clair River, Lake St. Clair, and the Detroit River.

Kneeling at the bottom of the fountain, her receiving basin considerably below that of Lake Erie, is the figure representing Lake Ontario, easternmost of the lakes. One of her arms points symbolically toward the distance. This lake is separated from her four sisters by the mighty cataract of Niagara Falls, over which the Niagara River, really a strait, tumbles on its course between Lakes Erie and Ontario. The drop-off from Erie to Ontario is 326 feet, approximately half of it at the falls and the rest through the gorge below them. Ships pass between the two lakes, around Niagara Falls, through the locks of the Welland Canal. The shortest of the lakes, 180 miles long and 53 miles wide, Ontario is much deeper than Erie, dropping off 738 feet at the deepest point. Lake Ontario is the doorway of the Great Lakes to the outer world. From her eastern tip the St. Lawrence River flows toward the Atlantic Ocean 1,150 miles away. Hence the pointing arm of the statue.

The sculptor caught a fundamental fact about the Great Lakes. They are like a series of descending stairsteps, their water draining eastward from Lake Superior through to Lake Ontario and thence toward the Atlantic Ocean. From Duluth, Minnesota, at the western tip of Lake Superior to the Atlantic a ship travels 2,314 miles, more than the length of the Mediterranean Sea, through the Soo Locks, down Lake Huron, past Detroit into Lake Erie, through the Welland Canal into Lake Ontario, and then down the St. Lawrence. Many Great Lakes ships are land-locked, however. They are too big to get through the locks of the Welland Canal and St. Lawrence Seaway, and so are destined to spend their entire lives on the four western lakes.

How much water is stored in the Great Lakes? Enough, if spread out, to cover the entire continental United States to a depth of fifteen feet! They have a total water surface of 95,180 square miles, equivalent to the combined size of five European countries, Portugal, Switzerland, Belgium, Denmark, and the Netherlands.

Such a mammoth sheet of water, carved up into five segments that are held together by four narrow connecting necks, is full of whims and moods; as unpredictable as a young girl in love, as the old-time ship captains say. In summer the surface can be so smooth that it looks like a mirror. But when the Arctic wind comes roaring out of the northeast on a dark December day the dirty gray waters are whipped into tumultuous white-capped seas that have sent hundreds of boats and thousands of men to their deaths. The waves surge thirty feet high, striking the long ships *chop, chop, chop* in quick succession like a boxer slamming jabs at his opponent's jaw. The seas hit faster than the rolling waves of the ocean and are as deadly. Water freezes on a ship's sides, shrouding the struggling vessel in a white blanket of ice from bow to stern.

The greatest fury of the lakes in recorded history occurred on November 9, 1913, a Sunday. A roaring blizzard born in Lake Superior swept across the lakes and over the land. Shipping on Lake Huron caught its brunt. Snow-laden winds thundered across the water at sixty to eighty miles an hour without pause. The temperature plummeted below zero. Snow whipped against the bodies of sailors struggling to keep their ships afloat, piling twenty-two inches deep on land. When the storm had passed, ten ships had been sunk, several of them large ore carriers, and a score of others driven ashore. Breakwaters were smashed. Towering waves had eroded great gaps in the sandy shorelines. On that dreadful day 235 sailors lost their lives. Few ocean storms have ever exacted such a toll.

Not only are the Great Lakes the scene of drastic and often tragic weather, they influence the weather experienced by much of the northeastern United States and southeastern Canada.

In winter, the Great Lakes usually are warmer than the air above them. When a cold weather front moves across the lakes from the northwest, it is affected by the rising warmth and moisture. This results in frequent snowstorms on the eastern edges of the lakes. Two notable snow belts caused by this effect are across northwestern Indiana and southwestern Michigan, for a distance of about forty miles inland at the southeast corner of Lake Michigan; and around Buffalo, at the eastern tip of Lake Erie.

A coating of ice makes the tanker *Mercury* look like a ghost ship. The *Mercury* left Superior, Wisconsin, on January 5, 1972, the latest sailing date in the port's 100-year history before ice closed it for the winter.

Since the prevailing winds cross the lakes from west to east, cities on the western shores of the lakes tend to get less snow than those on or near the eastern shores. Often, however, the cities on the eastern sides are warmer in winter than the cities farther south, because the moisture picked up from the lakes creates a cloud cover that moderates the temperature.

Generally, winter temperatures on the land around the Great Lakes, and to the east of them, are less severe than those in the territory to the west at the same latitude, because of the water's influence.

Among the phenomena of the Great Lakes is a strange condition called a seiche. A persistent wind from one direction or a large difference in barometric pressure on one portion of a lake causes the waters of the lake to swish back and forth like the water in a bathtub. Water is forced to one end of the lake, piling up there while the level at the other end of the lake may drop as much as eight feet within minutes. Lake Erie is especially susceptible to seiche waves.

The effect resembles a tidal wave at sea. Cold water at the bottom of the lake is sucked to the surface and the surface water drawn deep down. This causes chilling changes in temperature along the shore, perhaps twenty degrees, and disturbs the fish, different species of which seek underwater levels where the temperature is to their liking, according to the season of the year. The unexpected force of a seiche can cause tragedy, as at Chicago in 1954, when a huge seiche swept down Lake Michigan, killing seven persons on a pier when it hit the structure.

These, then, are the Great Lakes. Like small oceans in many ways, they even have tides, but never more than three inches. Still, they are unlike the oceans in important respects. They are fresh water, not salt; almost landlocked, yet carrying ships from their harbors to ports around the world. They teem with life, on the surface and below, yet there are remote rocky places where the shore looks almost as it did when the last Ice Age glacier withdrew from the land nearly thirty thousand years ago. In fact, it is the Ice Age that created the Great Lakes.

2

Stones and Bones

A workman digging an artificial pond in the spacious backyard of Federal Judge Joseph Sam Perry in Glen Ellyn, a northwestern suburb of Chicago, jabbed his shovel into the clay and had a surprise. Thud, the shovel blade struck something hard. His first thought was, "I've hit a big rock." Scraping with the blade, he realized that even though the white object was buried under several feet of dirt it couldn't be a rock, because it was too long and thin.

When he pried the object loose, he found that it was a bone, the biggest bone he had ever seen. What kind of an animal had it come from? And how did it happen to be buried there?

Geologists from nearby Wheaton College came to look and brought along excavating equipment. They dug up more bones, one of them a tusk eight and a half feet long, until they determined that the animal in Judge Perry's backyard was a mastodon. Testing by the radiocarbon method showed that this relic of prehistoric days had been trapped in the mud eleven thousand years ago. Now, by the chance stroke of a shovel, its bones were brought to light again in the midst of a modern American suburb.

The skull of the mastodon unearthed at Glen Ellyn, Illinois.

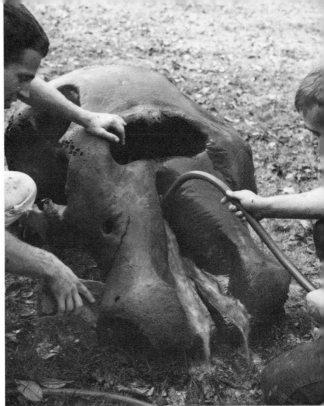

Curious girls examine the lower jaw of the mastodon unearthed at Glen Ellyn, Illinois. Other bones lie on each side of the jaw, and ribs in front. The reconstructed mastodon is on permanent display at Wheaton College.

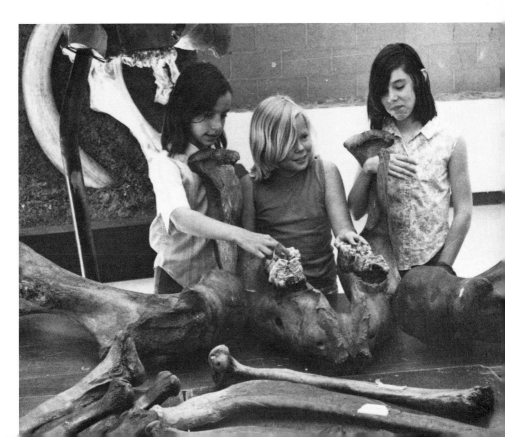

What an animal it had been! Resembling an elephant, it was nine and a half feet high, more than fifteen feet long, and weighed five to six tons. This huge creature, and hundreds like him, had roamed the pine forest that covered the land where Chicago stands, his massive teeth munching on branches of shrubs and trees. As he rumbled along a steep hillside, he somehow fell into the deep water of a lake that once covered the area around the judge's home. His bones sank into the soft bottom and, thus preserved from the air, did not disintegrate as the centuries passed. Slowly the lake filled with mud and plant material until it disappeared. Its dry bed formed the land on which the city developed.

Mastodons vanished from the earth about eight thousand years ago—a long time, but only a fraction of a minute, relatively speaking, in the way geologists calculate time. The Perry mastodon was almost a modern animal by geologic standards. Massive changes had occurred to the earth in the Great Lakes region during the tens of thousands of years that passed before the mastodons appeared. The Great Lakes as we know them are not much older than the bones of Judge Perry's backyard inhabitant.

Far back in time all the Great Lakes area was at the bottom of an ocean. Gradually the sea water retreated and the land emerged. On top of the bedrock formed when the earth was created, layers of sedimentary rock were built up from deposits in the ocean, containing fossil remnants of undersea creatures whose bodies had sunk into the ooze. Reefs of coral, similar to that found in the South Pacific, grew where Illinois prairies now stand. This ancient sea also deposited salt beds, especially in Michigan. Deep under Detroit there is a deposit of salt so huge that it can supply the world's needs for hundreds of years. While the city's millions go about their business far above, miners using electrically powered dump trucks haul twenty-ton loads of rock salt from mine shafts to a crusher.

Parts of this rocky overcoat that the earth acquired were softer than the rest and were eroded into troughs and valleys. Geologists believe that some of these valleys may have existed approximately where the Great Lakes stand today.

About a million years ago, the Northern Hemisphere of the earth began to grow colder. Snows that fell during the winter failed to melt in the spring because the temperature was so low, and soon another winter's snows accumulated on top of them. This was the beginning of the Ice Age. As the snow and ice piled higher in the north, the edge of the ice sheet moved relentlessly southward, forming as advancing wall of ice. Like a mammoth bulldozer it leveled hills in its path. Valleys were filled with dirt, rocks and trees were pushed ahead. Boulders imbedded in the moving ice gouged deep indentations into the bedrock and sedimentary deposits over which they were dragged. These marks are still visible in places where the bedrock has been exposed by modern quarrying. Some of the debris was pushed hundreds of miles and packed down more than a hundred feet thick atop the rock. A copper boulder scraped loose from its source in the copper deposits of the Upper Peninsula of northern Michigan was found 450 miles to the south, in Northern Illinois, and is on exhibit at the Field Museum of Natural History in Chicago.

The ice that spread south over the Great Lakes region may have been more than a mile thick at times, crushing down the surface of the earth.

Four times the ice advanced southward, driving animal life before it. Hundreds of thousands of years passed as the frozen blanket advanced, retreated, and advanced again. Water to create the ice caps was drawn from the oceans, which dropped to levels so low that land bridges were formed between continents. Over such a causeway animals and primitive man crossed and recrossed between Asia and North America.

During each period when the ice withdrew to northern Canada, foliage and animal life returned to the Great Lakes area; apparently the climate in those periods between glaciers was warmer than it is today.

The last of the four caps, known as the Wisconsin Ice Age, is responsible for gouging out the Great Lakes. At its furthest ad-

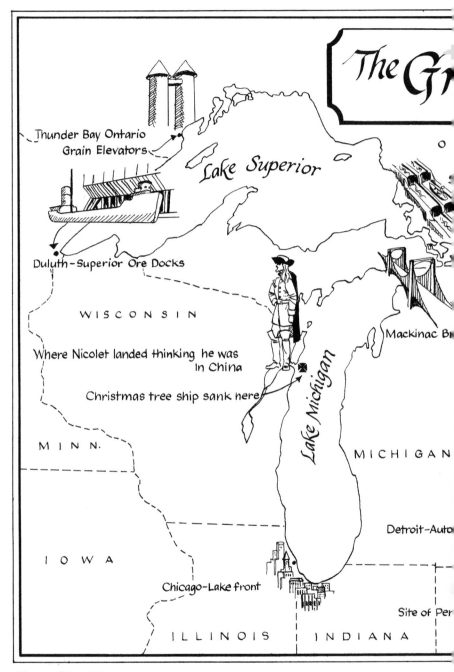

Thunder Bay Ontario
Grain Elevators

Lake Superior

The Gr

Duluth-Superior Ore Docks

WISCONSIN

Where Nicolet landed thinking he was
In China

Christmas tree ship sank here

Mackinac Br

MINN.

Lake Michigan

MICHIGAN

IOWA

Detroit-Auto

Chicago-Lake front

Site of Per

ILLINOIS   INDIANA

Map by Salem Tamer

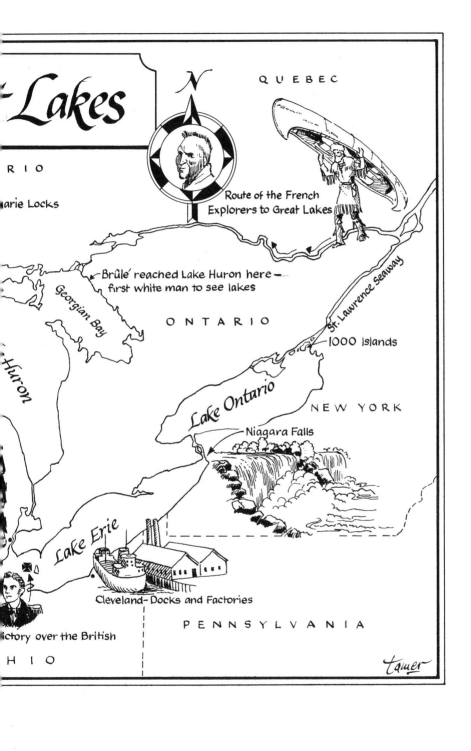

Lakes

QUEBEC

N

Route of the French
Explorers to Great Lakes

arie Locks

R I O

Georgian Bay

Brûlé reached Lake Huron here —
first white man to see lakes

O N T A R I O

St. Lawrence Seaway

1000 Islands

Huron

Lake Ontario

N E W Y O R K

Niagara Falls

Lake Erie

Cleveland-Docks and Factories

ctory over the British

P E N N S Y L V A N I A

H I O

Tamer

vance about thirty thousand years ago, the Wisconsin ice sheet reached central Ohio, Indiana, and Illinois and covered all of New York. Lines of low hills called moraines, consisting of debris pushed ahead of the ice sheet, mark its outer boundaries and are still visible today.

Eventually the ice began a slow retreat as the weather warmed. Water from the melting glacier collected in the ancient valleys, which had been dug deeper and wider by the gouging action of the Wisconsin ice sheet and now were being gradually exposed as the glacier withdrew. These deep, water-filled depressions became the Great Lakes. Still visible on hills at some points around the lakes are remnants of beach lines created when the water levels were much higher than they are today. Hundreds of smaller lakes in Michigan and Wisconsin were formed similarly at the same time.

After the shrinking of the ice sheet had exposed the lower sections of the Great Lakes, the ice cap still covered Lake Ontario and the eastern corner of Lake Erie. An ice plug filled the Straits of Mackinac and the outlet from Lake Superior. Water from Lake Erie drained eastward across New York State along the valley that was to be followed thousands of years later by the Erie Canal, and down the Hudson River valley into the Atlantic Ocean.

The waters of newly formed Lake Michigan overflowed the low land barrier that lies behind present-day Chicago and drained to the south into the Mississsippi River and the Gulf of Mexico. For awhile water from partially opened Lake Huron poured to the southwest across Michigan and then into the Mississippi.

As the centuries passed and the glacial retreat continued, the ice that covered Lake Ontario to a depth of several hundred feet melted away. The St. Lawrence River valley was uncovered, opening a watercourse from Lake Ontario into the Atlantic Ocean.

With its burden of ice removed the earth's surface expanded, much as a pillow rises when the sleeper's head is removed. This created the final shape of the Great Lakes. Also, it forced the water to drain from Lake Superior through Lake Huron and eastward through Lake Erie, rather than south through Lake Michigan into the Mississippi River.

A low rise of land across northern Illinois, Indiana, and Ohio, a few miles inland from Lake Michigan and Lake Erie, is all that keeps those lakes from draining south into the Mississippi River system today. Indeed, at one point in South Bend, Indiana, water poured from a bucket will divide and flow into two different drainage systems, some drops eventually reaching the Gulf of Mexico and others, the Atlantic Ocean.

The glacial age may not be ended yet. We may be living in another between-glaciers period, after which the ice sheet that now covers the Arctic areas could spread south across Canada and the northern United States just as the previous ones did. Only this time it would smash the cities that men have built. If the present average temperature dropped just 5 degrees Centigrade, scientists have calculated, the Ice Age would return.

When the accumulated waters from the four western lakes found a new outlet from Lake Erie to Lake Ontario, and thence down the St. Lawrence to the sea, they began pouring with a rumble like thunder over the sheer limestone ledge we know as Niagara Falls. This ledge is the most spectacular natural phenomenon of the entire Great Lakes shoreline. The Indians regarded it with superstitious awe.

From the moment it was first seen by a white man, Father Louis Hennepin, the Franciscan priest who accompanied Robert Cavelier, Sieur de La Salle, into the Great Lakes wilderness in 1678, Niagara Falls has been one of the renowned scenic wonders of the world. Trudging up the Niagara River gorge from Lake Ontario, Father Hennepin heard the roar of the falls, then stared in amazement at the tumult of water tumbling over the ledge through a curtain of spray. On his left he saw the sheet of water known as the American Falls; on the right, separated by an island, the deep horseshoe curve of the Canadian Falls. The doughty priest was not only a brave explorer but a mighty storyteller whose tales grew larger the more he repeated them.

"This marvelous waterfall is 600 feet high," he reported to his superiors in France. His enthusiasm overcame his accuracy; Niagara Falls actually is about 160 feet high from the brink of the precipice to the churning whirlpool at the bottom. From the base of the falls the water rushes through the gorge to Lake Ontario. The Niagara River drops the 326 feet between the levels of Lake Erie and Lake Ontario in thirty miles.

Niagara is an Indian word, meaning "Thunder of the Waters." A legend exists that Indians who once lived in the area considered the waterfall to be the voice of the Great Spirit and offered sacrifices to it. As the story goes, each spring the tribe's fairest maiden was placed in a canoe of white birch with an offering of flowers and foods and sent over the cataract to her death, to please the Great Spirit.

Niagara Falls, as depicted in Father Hennepin's book about his explorations which was published in 1699. He was the first white man to see the falls.

The *Maid of the Mist* near the foot of the American portion of Niagara Falls. Passengers wear raincoats and hats to keep dry while on this exciting ride.

Niagara Falls has been an attraction for tourists almost from colonial days. People travel from long distances to watch in fascination. Somehow the waterfall became a popular destination for honeymooners. For many decades newly married couples have gone to Niagara to gaze at the falls and into each other's eyes. Visitors ride on a little boat, *Maid of the Mist*, that edges close to the cataract. Huddled together on deck in raincoats issued to them, they feel dwarfed by the roaring deluge tumbling ahead of them. Trips also can be made by elevator down to the base of the falls from both the American and Canadian sides.

One day a few years before the Civil War a wiry French daredevil, Jean Francois Blondin, arrived at Niagara Falls and announced that he would give the spectators a thrill. He would walk across the deadly churning whirlpool below the falls on a tightrope. Such daring was hard to believe, to walk thirteen hundred feet across the gorge on a single strand of cable with instant death waiting far below if his foot slipped.

Crowds lined both shores on June 30, 1859, when Blondin set out from the American side. To balance himself he carried a pole thirty-eight feet long weighing forty-five pounds. Wiggling the pole with his hands to keep his equilibrium, he stepped cautiously out onto the cable. An expectant *Ahh* arose from the crowd. One hundred feet out from the American shore, Blondin sat down on the cable. He stretched out on his back, balancing the pole above him. He arose and stood on one foot. Halfway across, he surprised the onlookers with another stunt. The *Maid of the Mist* having steamed into position below him, he dropped a rope to her deck, pulled up a bottle and drank from it, then walked steadily on across to the Canadian shore. The crowds rewarded him with a shower of money.

Most men would have been satisfied to survive such an ordeal, but Blondin kept adding new flourishes on subsequent trips. He pushed a wheelbarrow ahead of him across the wire from the Canadian side to the American. He made the crossing at night. In those days before electric light, his only illumination was a flickering railroad engine headlight on each shore, but their beams were not bright enough to reach the middle of the torrent. Growing braver and braver, the acrobat made the quarter-mile trip blindfolded. Then, almost incredibly, he walked across the chasm backward!

In his most daring trip, Blondin walked the cable carrying another man pickaback. If Blondin was brave, his passenger, who was his manager Harry Colcord, could only be called foolhardy. He gambled his life on Blondin's sure-footedness and strength, and almost lost.

Seven times Colcord had to dismount and balance on the wire, clinging to Blondin while the acrobat rested. Their combined weight made the cable sag dangerously, so on the second half of

Artist's conception of Jean Francois Blondin walking a tightrope across the Niagara Falls gorge in 1859. The original of this picture was a brightly colored lithograph.

the trip Blondin was climbing uphill. At one point the weary Blondin put one foot on a guy wire, which had been strung out from the shore at an angle to keep the cable from swaying horizontally. As he rested part of his weight on the guy wire, it broke. For frantic moments, Blondin wiggled the long pole, fighting to regain his balance while Colcord hung helplessly on his back. The men teetered to one side, then the other, their lives hanging in the balance. With excruciating slowness, the acrobat righted himself and struggled up the wire the remaining few hundred feet to safety. A thunderous shout of relief arose from the terrified crowd.

Another breed of daredevils were fascinated by Niagara Falls, people who risked their lives by going over the falls in a barrel. The first one to do so was a woman. Quite a heavy woman, too, weighing 160 pounds. Her name was Mrs. Anna Edson Taylor. She designed a long, steel-bound barrel, placing a small blacksmith's anvil at the bottom to prevent it from bobbing end over end. On October 24, 1901, Mrs. Taylor crawled into her barrel and the lid was screwed on. The fragile craft was pushed into the Niagara River about three-fourths of a mile above the Horseshoe Falls. Bobbing in the foam of the rapids, the barrel approached the precipice. Onlookers lost sight of the barrel as it disappeared into the sheet of spray rising from the brink. Then they saw it bounding in the whirlpool below. The barrel was intact, but was Mrs. Taylor still alive? Floating downstream close to shore, the barrel was pulled to safety, the top opened, and there was Mrs. Taylor seasick and bruised but otherwise unharmed. For a woman forty-three years old, it had been quite a ride!

This kind of crazy adventure no longer is permitted at Niagara Falls. Anyone who attempted stunts like Blondin's tightrope walks or Mrs. Taylor's barrel ride would be stopped by police. Today's visitors to the falls must be satisfied with the awesome sight and sound of the water, which should be enough for anyone.

While the towering limestone barrier creates a famous scenic view, also for many years it prevented the movement of ships

A view of Niagara Falls from the bottom of Bridal Veil Falls on the American side shows the tremendous power of the tumbling water.

from the other four Great Lakes into Lake Ontario and the St. Lawrence River. It was like a plug in a bottle. Since ships couldn't go over the falls in safety, a way had to be found to go around them. Actually, a couple of ships did go over the falls. In an almost unbelievably cruel stunt in 1827, a promoter trying to make money from thrill-seekers loaded the old wooden schooner *Michigan* with a camel, a bear, an elk, and several dogs, like a miniature Noah's Ark, and sent it drifting over the cataract. The ship splintered to bits on the rocks below. All the animals were killed while large crowds of spectators, who had paid for their vantage points, looked on. Another promoter of the same period sent a burning wooden ship over the falls like a flaming torch.

Ships now bypass the falls and travel between Lakes Erie and Ontario through the Welland Canal. Since Lake Ontario is lower than Lake Erie, vessels must descend to it through a series of locks, like a flight of watery steps. The Welland Canal was opened in 1829, a narrow, primitive waterway by current standards but an almost revolutionary boon to shipping at the time. A ship passed through forty wooden locks in the 26-mile length,

Early photo of the Old Welland Canal, St. Catharines, Ontario, taken in 1889

Shipping at Port Dalhousie, Old Welland Canal, 1885

each lock being opened and closed by hand. The canal could handle only shallow vessels with an eight-foot draft. As ships grew larger the canal was rebuilt four times to accomodate them. Now it handles large cargo vessels from Europe that have come in from the Atlantic Ocean through the St. Lawrence Seaway.

Niagara Falls and gorge provide men with more than scenery. A huge amount of electricity is generated in the power plants on both American and Canadian shores. Water is drawn from the swift stream and returned to it after turning the wheels of the turbines. Power lines carry the current to homes and industrial plants for hundreds of miles around.

The limestone ridge over which the cataract pours lies on top of soft shale and sandstone which were laid down when the ancient ocean covered the region. As water rushes over the hard limestone lip of the falls, it swirls back to wear away the softer stone underneath. Thus undercut, the limestone ledge chips off. When Father Hennepin saw the waterfall three hundred years ago, it was several hundred feet downstream from its present site. For many years the falls retreated upstream more than four feet a year; modern engineering work has slowed this to less than two feet a year. Eventually the falls will reach Lake Erie. Then they will dwindle into a series of rapids instead of a waterfall. The danger isn't exactly imminent, however. Geologists believe Niagara Falls still has about five thousand years of life.

3

The Indians Came First

Étienne Brûlé had lived through two raw and hungry winters in the cluster of huts forming the French settlement which huddled below the massive cliff of Quebec, at the edge of the St. Lawrence River. These had been harsh times for the party of young men who had sailed up the river from their native France with Samuel de Champlain in 1608. All but eight of them had died that first winter, of scurvy. But Brûlé proved himself to be of a stronger breed than most, and more adventurous, too.

Champlain's tiny colony was isolated in the New World. Downstream on the broad St. Lawrence lay the Atlantic Ocean, a perilous passage to home for a twenty-ton wooden sailing vessel but at least a known world. Upstream toward the heart of the continent lay mystery.

What little the French knew about inland America came from their fumbling conversations with the almost naked Algonquin Indians who wandered into Quebec in the summers. To the Frenchmen, the natives looked a strange lot. Their faces were painted in brilliant colors, their bronze bodies covered with tattooed designs. At first the Indians and the fair-skinned men had no words in common. As they learned to exchange ideas with gestures and a few words, the Indians told of large lakes, rapids, and waterfalls lying to the west. How far? Many days' journey by canoe.

Young Brûlé was fascinated by the Indians and their tales. He wanted to see the country for himself. His opportunity came in the summer of 1610 when a party of Algonquins came down the St. Lawrence to trade their furs for French knives and weapons. Champlain struck a bargain with the Algonquin chief—he would take a young Indian youth back to France if the Indians would take a young man of his party into the inland wilderness. He choose Étienne Brûlé, then eighteen years old.

"Go live with the Indians," he told Étienne. "Learn their language and their customs. See the great lakes they tell about."

When the cavalcade of Indians shoved off from Quebec in late summer, Brûlé had a place in one of the birchbark canoes, putting his weight to a paddle like his native companions. The half-dozen men in each canoe paddled upstream against the current until they passed the place on the northern shore where someday the great port of Montreal would stand.

Étienne Brûlé had started on an adventure that would last the rest of his life.

For the next twenty-two years he lived among the Indians. He returned to Quebec only rarely to report and to refresh himself for a few days with such memories of European life as could be found in that remote French outpost. He did as Champlain instructed him. He abandoned French clothing for an animal-skin loincloth, moccasins and, in winter, a loose jacket of bearskin and leggings. He learned to talk the Indians' dialects, to sleep on the bare ground in their flea-infested huts of sticks and bark. Concealing his distaste, he learned to satisfy his hunger by dipping into their communal dish of sagamite, a gooey concoction of crushed corn into which chunks of meat, fish, and a leavening of bear fat had been stirred. On celebration days, when the Indians killed and cooked one of the dogs that hung around their camps, he ate his share.

Brûlé is a shadowy figure in history. Unlike many later explorers he never recorded his deeds on paper. They are known only through the accounts of Champlain and others. We know that he was the first white man to look upon three of the five Great Lakes —Ontario, Huron, and Superior.

The wilderness into which he headed stretched out interminably to the west, more than a thousand miles of heavy, gloomy forest and rapid rivers broken by open fields and rocks, forming a setting for those blue jewels, the Great Lakes.

For perhaps twelve thousand years Indians had been living around these lakes, yet their primitive existence had made hardly a mark on the surface of the area. The Great Lakes region was almost untouched virgin forest, crisscrossed by trails worn by many generations of moccasined feet. Brûlé could not have guessed that the white tide that was to follow him eventually would

No one knows what ancient people built the Great Serpent Mound in Adams County, Ohio. The civilization no longer existed when explorers came to the area.

drive the Indians from their homes and almost wipe out their descendants.

Nobody knows for certain when the first Indians came upon the huge inland lakes during their wanderings in search of food. Probably they did so before the Great Lakes assumed their final shape as the Ice Age ended. Because the Indians could not write, they left no record of their history. Tales of the past handed down from generation to generation became overlaid with legend and fanciful storytelling, so that it is impossible to separate fact from imagination.

Our knowledge of the first humans to live around the lakes comes from intricate detective work performed by scientists. At widely scattered points, fragmentary remnants of ancient Indian civilization have been uncovered—in twenty-foot deep pits in the iron country of Michigan's Upper Peninsula, far under the soil of Wisconsin and Ontario, and occasionally exposed on the surface.

Geologists studying the layers of soil and rock have been able to put approximate dates to the earth's history during and after the Ice Age. When the trunk of a tree is found in a certain layer of soil, for example, they can estimate the date it was buried by use of the radiocarbon testing method. If crude Indian spearpoints and tools of chipped stone are found at the same level as the tree, it follows that Indians of a certain cultural stage lived there at the same time. Using these methods of fact-finding and deduction, archeologists and geologists paint a picture.

Pre-historic men from eastern Asia wandered across the land bridge that linked Asia and North America when the Pacific Ocean was at a low level during the Ice Age. This land bridge stood where the Bering Strait separates Alaska and Siberia today. As thousands of years passed, descendants of these first hunters moved down the Pacific Coast and eastward. They could not penetrate into the Great Lakes area, however, because it was buried beneath the massive ice cap. When the glaciers retreated and the weather warmed, the newly exposed lands sprouted grass and then forests. The lumbering mastodons, deer, elk, and other animals followed.

These copper spear points were found in Marathon and Shawano Counties in Wisconsin.

Close behind them came the first Indians from the south. They hunted the mastodons with long spears to which they attached sharp-pointed heads chipped from stone. The circumstances in which some of these spearpoints have been found convince scientists that Indians were in the southern portion of the Great Lakes region by 10,000 B.C. Indeed, that mastodon whose remains were found in Judge Perry's backyard may have been fleeing clumsily from early Indian hunters when it fell into the ancient lake and died.

Gradually the Indians increased in number and moved north behind the retreating ice. Their skill in fashioning weapons and utensils grew, as can be seen by a study of the relics preserved in museums. One group known as the Old Copper Indians who lived in the Upper Peninsula of Michigan from about 5000 to 2000 B.C. found the copper deposits that the white men were to mine so extensively thousands of years later. These primitive men dug deep pits for the copper and shaped it into simple tools. Then, mysteriously, they died out. When Brûlé and other white men reached Lake Superior they heard vague tales from the Indians about copper. These natives were making virtually no effort to mine it, however, and other tribes a few hundred miles to the east had no knowledge of metal at all.

It has been estimated that by the time the white men came, more than 100,000 Indians were living around the Great Lakes. Spread over such a large area, that really wasn't a great number, less than one person per square mile. Life was concentrated around the lakes and along rivers because most Indian travel was by water. The Indians north of the Great Lakes, and around Lake Superior, survived mostly by hunting and fishing. Those close to the shores obtained much of their food by farming, scratching the fertile soil with stone tools and growing corn, beans, and squashes. In the winter they went on hunting expeditions.

Frequently the tribes warred among themselves. This usually was hit-and-run warfare on the enemy's villages, rather than sustained battles for conquest of territory. Wielding their tomahawks, they swept down on rival villages stealthily at night, killed their foes in their sleep if possible, seized captives, and disappeared into the forest. Once at a safe distance they tortured some prisoners to death. They adopted others into their tribes, usually at the request of the tribal women, to replace men of their own group who had been lost in battle. Life was crude and harsh, to the minds of the French priests who circulated among the Indians, and frequently illogical. They found that Indians who were jovial and friendly at one moment could be cruel and vicious under other circumstances.

When the Indians of Étienne Brûlé's party had carried their canoes around the rapids above Montreal, they reached a point where the Ottawa River flows into the St. Lawrence from the northwest. Instead of following the St. Lawrence westward into Lake Ontario, as might have been expected, they turned their canoe prows up the much smaller Ottawa.

This turn to the right was to influence the history of Great Lakes discovery for nearly a century.

Today, ships follow the natural course of the Great Lakes waterway up the St. Lawrence into Lake Ontario, on through Lakes Erie and Huron to Lake Michigan or Lake Superior. Brûlé's Algonquin companions did not dare follow that route because of the deadly state of war between them and the Iroquois Indians. The five tribes, or nations, of the Iroquois family lived in New York State and along the southeastern shores of Lake Erie. They controlled the southern shore of Lake Ontario and the eastern end of Lake Erie. Had the northern Indians tried to travel by the Lake Ontario-Lake Erie route, they would have been in the country of their hated, and much stronger, enemies. So they made a long, difficult detour far to the north.

Since the French happened to come into the New World up the St. Lawrence River, their first contacts were with the Algonquins and their neighbors, the Hurons. Having made peace with them, the French automatically became their allies against the Iroquois. For many decades, therefore, the French were forced to follow the detour up the Ottawa River, which came to be known as the "fur traders' highway." They avoided Lake Erie entirely.

Brûlé and his party, heading up the Ottawa, repeatedly had to get out of the canoes and, plunging into the swift water, pull them by ropes through the rapids. They were attacked by masses of fierce mosquitoes. After passing the scenic bluff where the present city of Ottawa stands, they carried their canoes across land on a series of portages, thirty-five altogether, to Lake Nipissing. From there they paddled down the French River until they reached Georgian Bay, the northeast corner of Lake Huron. There, for the first time, a white man saw one of the Great Lakes.

Brûlé seems to have been fearless. Once he made a trip on foot through the forested Iroquois country of western New York to visit a band of potential allies for his Huron friends. While walking the hundreds of miles back toward the Huron territory, along obscure trails to avoid the Iroquois, he almost starved. In desperation he walked into an Iroquois village, gambling that he could talk them into accepting him. Instead, they bound him to a pole and tortured him. The Indians pulled out his beard hair by hair and ripped off his fingernails. With hot sticks they poked holes in his

Rafts of sawed lumber float in the Ottawa River behind the Parliament Buildings in Ottawa, 1890. French explorers paddled their canoes up the river past this spot on their way to the Great Lakes.

Parliament Buildings at Ottawa, the capital of Canada. Étienne Brûlé and other French explorers followed the canoe route up the Ottawa River past this site, which overlooks the river at the rear.

flesh. One of them grabbed at the religious medal he wore around his neck.

"Touch that and you will die. And so will your family!" Brûlé warned.

Almost at that moment, as he later reported to Champlain, a weird thing happened. While the Indians played their cruel game of torture with him, black clouds had been gathering. Lightning flashed and thunder shook the earth.

Terrified, the superstitious Indians drew away. The white man had warned them, and see what had happened. This man with the shiny medal around his neck was supernatural. Hastily, they freed him. Then, to get themselves right with this representative of the Great Spirit, they feasted him and provided an escort to the Huron country.

Although skilled in the crafts of the forest the Indians were so ignorant in other matters that it is difficult for us to comprehend how simple their life was. Brûlé and other Frenchmen who lived with the Indians found that they had no metal and had to make their hatchets and knives of stone. They had no wheeled vehicles. Traveling through the forest, the Indians carried everything on their backs—the women's backs, actually. The lordly braves carried only their weapons. They made fire by rubbing a piece of soft wood with hard wood. Some tribes lived in wigwams of branches covered with hides or bark. Others built longhouses where several families lived, each with its own fire. Holes were left at the top to let out the smoke, but so much of it was trapped inside that the houses had a pungent odor.

Cleanliness, as the Europeans knew it—and even the European concept of cleanliness in the 1600's was primitive by our standards—didn't exist among the Indians. The more meticulous men among the French missionary priests were so disturbed by the odors and dirt around the native villages that they had difficulty in eating at first. The Indians paid little heed to the vermin that crawled around their homes. Not so the Frenchmen, whose zeal for converting the natives to Christianity was severely tested by the biting and scratching they had to endure. At times tenderfoot priests went off into the forest alone to sleep, hoping to escape the insects.

The Great Lakes Indians favored the sweat bath, a primitive version of the modern sauna. The site of this ordeal, which is what it really should be called, was a small structure six or seven feet high into which seven or eight persons could crowd. Mats and furs covered the top to keep out the fresh air. On the ground in the bath house were placed stones heated to a high temperature in a fire. Over these stones water was poured. This sizzled into the air as clouds of steam. The atmosphere became so hot that the hardiest men almost fainted. To prevent anyone from passing out, the men, sweating profusely, threw water in each other's faces. When the heat became almost unbearable, the bathers ran out and plunged into a cold river nearby, splashing madly. It might seem that such a sudden and extreme change in temperature would make them ill. On the contrary, the method was used to treat illness and often seemed to work. Just getting the layers of dirt off the skin probably had a curative effect.

In the nights around the village fires, Brûlé heard many tales. The Indians lived intimately with nature and took their beliefs from it.

They had a legend about the creation of the earth. Before there was ground on which men could live, they believed, everything had been water. Upon this endless water a great wooden raft floated, bearing animals of all kinds. Leading them was the Great Hare. Several animals tried diving into the water in search of soil, but failed. Finally the muskrat made a deep, deep dive and came up clutching a grain of sand in his paw. Placed upon the raft, the grain multiplied wonderously to form a piece of land. When the animals died, the Great Hare caused the birth of men from their corpses. He did the same from the bodies of fish in the surrounding sea. Thus some Indians derived their origin from the bear, others from the moose, the deer, or the beaver. Their villages were named for the animals from which their people had come.

Life was especially hard for the Indian women. They did the work while the men hunted, fished, or smoked their pipes. In the

Tools used by the Great
Lakes Indians—drill points,
scraper, and knife.

Jar used by Great Lakes
Indians was found at Cass
City, Michigan.

Birchbark dish made by the Menominee Indians, Wisconsin.

fields of corn and beans, it was the women who hacked at the ground with stone tools to plant and cultivate the seeds. They carried wood for the fires and hauled water from the streams. No Indian man would touch woman's work.

Often during a heavy winter severe hunger plagued the Indians. A period of poor hunting or the failure of a village's crops led to starvation, because most of the tribes lacked a sense of the future. They lived from day to day. If there was an abundance of food they glutted themselves, not saving for tomorrow. They developed the ability to go long periods without food, from necessity. When their canoe caravans traveled along the edges of the Great Lakes, the men paddled for hours without a halt, nibbling only rarely from the skimpy supply of cold food each man carried.

The primitive men of the Great Lakes wilderness were fascinated by the things the white men brought with them and adopted them quickly, either by trading their furs or stealing. The Indians did not have the same sense of property ownership as the Europeans had. Gradually, guns replaced bows and arrows. The red men unfortunately soon learned the potency of the white man's whiskey. Guns and whiskey in the Indians' hands were to cause the death of many men in the next two centuries.

The white men acquired things from the Indians, too; things they still use today. Corn probably was the greatest contribution the Indians made to the rest of the world. Moccasins, the soft Indian footgear, still are a popular style. The canoe has been adopted for camping and fishing trips, although it is made of aluminum now instead of birchbark. Snowshoes came from the Indians, as did the game of lacrosse.

So did many names of cities, counties, rivers, and lakes. Everywhere in the states around the Great Lakes there are commonly used names that are anglicized versions of Indian words.

To keep track of the tribal names of the Indians and the places where the tribes lived around the Great Lakes is complicated business. Those whose names sound so romantic may have consisted of only a few thousand members. Some had names which were rendered in different ways when translated into French and English, and others moved from area to area to find safe havens after defeats in wars.

Black buckskin bag, quilled decoration, made by the Huron Indians about 1775.

It is sufficient for us to remember that the Algonquins and Hurons—later Wyandots—lived generally on the northern, or Canadian, side of the St. Lawrence River and the Great Lakes, as far west as Lake Huron. Beyond them were the Ottawas and, in the remote wilderness encircling Lake Superior, the Ojibwas or Chippewas. Wisconsin was populated by several tribes, the Winnebago, Sauk, Fox, Menominee, and Kickapoo. The Miamis and their relatives lived on the wooded flatlands of northern Illinois, Indiana, and Ohio. Michigan was populated mostly by the Potawatomis in the west and the Ottawas in the east, around Detroit. The Five Nations of the Iroquois—the Mohawks, Oneidas, Onondagas, Cayugas, Senacas, and, later, a sixth tribe, the displaced Tuscaroras—were to the east, south of the Great Lakes. Of these, the Mohawks, with the fiercest warriors, were the most politically advanced of all the Great Lakes tribes.

Although he traveled among other tribes, Brûlé spent most of his two decades in the wilderness among the Hurons. They were his friends, or so he thought. But it was they who killed him. His death while he was still a relatively young man was a grim example of the ways of these Indians. The Hurons turned against Brûlé in 1632, apparently after he was involved in a drunken brawl, tortured him to death, and, after boiling his body, ate it in a cannibal feast. The French priests reported other instances of cannibalism among the Hurons and Iroquois, although the practice was not followed among most other North American tribes.

From his birth in a small French farm town near Paris to his terrible death in the Canadian wilderness four thousand miles away, Brûlé's life had bridged the gap between two worlds. Behind him were to come first a trickle of other explorers, then a flood of European settlers who soon ruled the lands the Indians had called their own for so long.

4

La Salle's Grand Dream

From the dark edge of the forest on the east bank of the Niagara River a short distance above the falls, hostile Indians looked on and wondered, "What are the white men up to now?" They were mystified by the clatter of hammering and sawing, the clang of the blacksmith's forge—sounds they had never heard before. They weren't sure what was happening, but they didn't like it.

The place was a stump-covered clearing on the outskirts of modern Buffalo, the year 1679. Here a party of Frenchmen led by that dashing and imaginative adventurer, Robert Cavelier, Sieur de la Salle, was building a ship that would make history, the first to sail on the Great Lakes above the falls. This vessel La Salle hoped to make the main tool in his grandiose plan for an inland American empire.

Although they hesitated to attack because the French had guns, the Indians harassed the shipbuilders. They dashed into the clearing, howling and waving tomahawks. One came near the blacksmith, swinging his tomahawk as though to kill him.

"Get out of here!" the blacksmith shouted, as he snatched a red-hot iron bar from his fire. He jabbed it into the attacker, who ran screaming back into the forest.

As a young gentleman of France, LaSalle wears the long curls popular with men in the mid-1600's.

After many weeks, La Salle's men shoved their vessel into the Niagara River. La Salle named her the *Griffin* and had painted on the sail of her forward mast a picture of that mythological animal with the head and wings of an eagle and the body of a lion. The *Griffin* was sixty feet long and weighed forty-five tons, tiny in comparison to current lake ships but hundreds of times larger than the biggest Indian canoe.

On August 7, the *Griffin* spread her white sails and, catching the wind, slid from the river into Lake Erie. On her quarterdeck stood La Salle, in command of a crew of thirty-one. He was an imperious figure with a sharply boned nose, a thin, pointed mustache, and hair reaching to his shoulders. Haunted by debts and enemies back in Quebec, he saw this moment of sailing as the start of an adventure that would bring him fortune and France the possession of rich new lands. At his command the ship's five cannons were fired. Their roar terrified a band of Iroquois braves returning home from a raiding party deep into the midwestern prairies, a party of captive slaves herded before them.

Aboard the *Griffin* were La Salle's faithful and able lieutenant, Henry de Tonty, called "Tonty of the Iron Hand" because of the metal artificial hand that replaced one he had lost during a battle in Italy, and Father Hennepin.

Her canvas billowing in the fair summer breeze, the *Griffin* sailed the length of Lake Erie in three days and entered the long strait that links Lakes Erie and Huron. Father Hennepin wrote, "The country on both sides of this beautiful strait is adorned with fine open plains, and you can see numbers of stags, does, deer, bears, by no means fierce and very good to eat . . . swans in abundance." The idyllic land he described is where the massive automobile factories of Detroit stand today and, across the river, the buildings of Windsor, Ontario. The name Detroit, incidentally, comes from the French word for "strait."

When his ship sailed up into Lake Huron, La Salle was not the first white man to penetrate these areas. But he was first to go about exploring and fur-trading on such a large, well-organized scale. Not only did he gamble his life, but a fortune as well.

The men who came before him had had only their lives to risk, for to them earthly goods were of no importance, and they possessed nothing beyond the barest necessities. They were the black-robed Jesuit priests. Driven by a fervor to convert the Indians to Christianity, they suffered almost unendurable hardships as they plodded on sandal-clad feet through the wild country. Had they been of less faith and courage, they would have surrendered. The task of planting the Cross and teaching the Indians was discouraging, almost hopeless at times, and dangerous. The records of the Jesuits are filled with stories of these zealous men in tattered black robes who died in the wilderness.

Of these Jesuit missionary travelers, the best known is Jacques Marquette. History records Pére Marquette as the white man who discovered the Mississippi River. This deeply devout man probably would rather have been remembered for the number of In-

47

Portrait of Father Jacques Marquette, an explorer of the Great Lakes and first white man to see the Mississippi River.

dians whom he rather precariously converted to Christianity. His memory is preserved in the name of Marquette University at Milwaukee, a railroad, a city in Michigan, and innumerable schools and streets.

After a period at a remote mission on Lake Superior, Marquette built a log chapel at the Straits of Mackinac. From there in May, 1673, he and Louis Jolliet, accompanied by five other men, set out westward along the northern shore of Lake Michigan in two canoes. Their paddling took them along much the same course that Jean Nicolet had followed thirty-nine years earlier, when he thought he was about to reach China. Each night the party pulled the canoes ashore, overturned them, and made camp around a fire on the forested banks of the lake. They visited a village of Menominee Indians and told them of their plans to hunt for the Mississippi, about which Indians had told them.

"Do not go there," the Menominees warned. "Every stranger who comes to the banks of the Great River is put to death by the men who live along its banks." They told of other perils: "There

48

are demons in the water that will swallow you and your canoes."

Not easily disturbed by the superstitions of the natives, Marquette and his party pushed ahead. They paddled their canoes up Green Bay, up the Fox River through Lake Winnebago in Wisconsin, and reached a great village of the Miamis.

These Indians, too, were friendly, perhaps because of the gifts they were given. The chiefs and elders gathered solemnly in a council to hear from Marquette and Jolliet of their plans and offered them guides. As the French party pushed up the Fox River among the marshes of wild rice, a guide halted them.

"Here," he said, pointing to the shore.

The men of the party dragged their canoes out of the water, packed the baggage on their backs, lifted the canoes onto their shoulders, and started walking. For a mile and a half they followed an ancient Indian portage route until they reached another river, the Wisconsin. They had crossed a low divide. The waters of the Fox up which they had come flowed northeast into the Great Lakes and ultimately into the Atlantic Ocean; those of the Wisconsin flowed southwest into the Mississippi and the far-away Gulf of Mexico.

Drifting down the quiet Wisconsin, one canoe behind the other, the Frenchmen seven days later found themselves entering the broad, swift current of the Mississippi, Father of the Waters. Marquette wrote in his journal that as he looked upon the river his heart was filled "with a joy which I cannot express."

Marquette and Jolliet steered their flimsy craft south a thousand miles down the Mississippi—a thousand miles of solitude, past the forested future site of St. Louis, past the mouths of the Missouri and Ohio Rivers, as far as the Arkansas River. Whenever they met a band of Indians, Marquette offered them the calumet, the pipe of peace, and then preached to them the word of God. Talking with Indians they met at the mouth of the Arkansas, they became convinced that the Mississsippi flowed into the Gulf of Mexico, not into the Pacific Ocean as some supposed.

They turned their canoes around for the strenuous upstream trip back to the Great Lakes, against the current. This time they

Signature of Louis Jolliet, who accompanied Marquette on his travels. Minus one "l," the city of Joliet, Illinois, is named for him.

went up the Illinois River and reached Lake Michigan through the mouth of the Chicago River, then paddled up the lake to the mission at Green Bay. They had completed a perilous trip of 2,500 miles in more than four months. The role of Jolliet in this adventure is commemorated by a city named in his honor, with the loss of one "l"—Joliet, Illinois.

Pére Marquette was a man of broken health by then, but of iron will. He was determined to keep his promise of returning to the Indians he had converted to Christianity on the Illinois prairie.

Late the next year he and two companions pushed their canoe into Lake Michigan's waves again, working their way down its shore to the mouth of the Chicago River. It was November and winter was upon them. Snow was falling. Sick again and weak, Marquette, with the help of his companions, built a rude cabin near the river's mouth, at a spot now overshadowed by Chicago's lake-front skyscrapers. After four shivering, lonely months, during which Marquette feared he was dying, the three men welcomed the signs of spring. In late March, 1675, they resumed their journey up the Chicago River into central Illinois.

When they reached the Indian villages, Pére Marquette was greeted with affection. At Easter he unfurled four large taffeta pieces, adorned with pictures of the Virgin, and preached to several thousand Indians in their own tongue. There may be doubt about how well the natives understood the religious mysteries he described but they were enthusiastic and he was deeply moved.

His sickness growing worse, and convinced that he would soon die, Marquette started the long canoe trip back to the only home he really knew, his mission at the Straits of Mackinac. He lay feebly in the canoe as his two companions drove it up the rivers to Chicago and then north along the eastern shore of Lake Michigan. Each night they carried him ashore. Halfway up the length of Michigan, near where Ludington stands, he could go no farther. The men built a flimsy shelter and there he died, praying almost until his final hour. His companions buried him in the forest.

But this was not to be the indomitable priest's last resting place. Two years later a band of Indians whom Marquette had converted to Christianity searched out his grave and in a funeral procession of nearly thirty canoes bore his remains to the chapel at the Straits of Mackinac. There, as white men and Indians prayed together, they were interred.

As La Salle sailed up Lake Huron toward the settlement at Mackinac aboard the *Griffin*, his dreams were quite different from those of Marquette, who had died four years earlier. The priest had sought converts; La Salle sought furs. The forests that surrounded the western Great Lakes were filled with wild animals. Beavers by the thousands built their dams along the streams. Far away in Europe, in the royal courts and among the wealthy, furs made from the pelts of these industrious, amphibious animals were in great demand as decorative garments. La Salle's plan was to collect furs from Indian trappers and to pay for them with bright cloth, metal tools, guns, whiskey, mirrors and other trinkets carried aboard the *Griffin*. He would send the fur-laden ship back east to unload, then bring another cargo of trading merchandise to the back country. Later, he would build another trading vessel on the Illinois River and run a similar trading operation up and down the Mississippi River.

The result he visualized would be a series of fortified trading posts in a great scimitar-like arc from eastern Canada through the Great Lakes and down to the Gulf of Mexico.

For La Salle, successful completion of the plan would mean great wealth. For France, it would mean political control of a huge area of inland America. With their own men controlling the waterways, and through alliances with their Indian trading partners, the French would keep the rival English colonies bottled up along the Atlantic coast.

All that stood in La Salle's way was the Great Lakes wilderness itself. Would it yield to his elaborate scheme?

Soon after the *Griffin* entered Lake Huron, great peril developed. The ship was passing Saginaw Bay when one of those furious gales for which Lake Huron is noted blew up with staggering violence. The vessel which had appeared so huge to the Indians seemed tiny and almost helpless. High, choppy waves tossed the vessel until it threatened to capsize. Scrambling up into the rigging, sailors hauled down the sails, and the *Griffin* was turned broadside to the shore, while La Salle sought in vain for a sheltered anchorage.

Frightened, the men huddled into the cabin below deck while the ship wallowed helplessly. La Salle strode in from outside, soaked, disheveled, and almost breathless. He, too, feared that they were doomed and told his men, "I commend this enterprise to God."

The entire company knelt around Father Hennepin in prayer and sang hymns. Invoking Saint Anthony of Padua as their protector, La Salle promised that if they survived, the first chapel he built when he reached the mouth of the Mississippi would be dedicated to that saint.

The *Griffin* did indeed ride out the storm safely. But the chapel in Louisiana never was built.

Their spirits regained, the crew sailed joyously on to the Straits of Mackinac. They fired their cannon as the *Griffin* anchored in the safe harbor and, to impress the natives further with his importance, La Salle strode ashore in his scarlet cloak with gold lace. Such grandeur far exceeded anything the most exalted Indian chief in his finest ceremonial garb had ever been able to achieve.

From Mackinac, La Salle sailed the *Griffin* along the path of

Nicolet and Marquette to Green Bay. Here his advance agents had gathered a large store of furs. Everything was going according to plan. Ignoring the advice of others in the party, La Salle decided to send the *Griffin* back through the lakes to Niagara with the furs while he continued the trip to the Mississippi River by canoe.

On a bright day in mid-September, the *Griffin* fired a farewell shot from a single cannon and departed on its long voyage, aided by a favorable westerly breeze. As it disappeared from the sight of La Salle and his men waving on the shore, the ship vanished forever. It was never heard from again. Apparently it sank in another lake storm, the first of scores of vessels that were to vanish mysteriously in the Great Lakes during the next three hundred years.

For La Salle, things rarely went right after that.

With fourteen men in four heavily laden canoes, one of which carried an iron forge, La Salle paddled down the west side of Lake Michigan, around the southern end past the future site of Chicago, and back up the eastern shore to the mouth of the St. Joseph River in Southern Michigan. Here he built Fort Miami as a rendezvous. Strengthened by reinforcements brought by Tonty from Mackinac, La Salle's party of thirty-three men in eight canoes paddled fifty miles up the wooded St. Joseph to the present site of South Bend, Indiana, where the river makes a big turn to the east.

Here they carried their canoes nearly five miles along an Indian portage across swampy land to a narrow ditch barely wide enough to hold the craft. They had crossed another of those low land barriers that divide the waters that drain into the Atlantic Ocean or the Gulf of Mexico and reached the headwater of the Kankakee River. This flows into the Illinois River, and the Illinois into the Mississippi. They followed this water route into Central Illinois, to the present city of Peoria, where they built Fort Crevecouer. The prairies along the route were thick with the remains of dead buffalo.

Recently, a South Bend business man tried to follow La Salle's

La Salle and his party carry their birchbark canoes over the portage from the St. Joseph River to the Kankakee River in 1679, crossing from the Great Lakes into the Mississippi River stream system. The site is at South Bend, Indiana.

route from the headwaters of the Kankakee in a fiberglass kayak. His nights sleeping on the river banks were disturbed by cows and trucks. In five and a half days of paddling, he struggled through weeds, around dams, past logs, and over rocks. He covered 170 miles before giving up. Friends drove him back home in three and a half hours.

The second ship of La Salle's great plan began to take shape in Illinois. But necessary parts had been lost on the *Griffin*. La Salle realized he must take a desperate risk.

"I must go back to Canada to get what we need," he told Tonty. "You keep the camp here until I return."

What followed was a journey of almost unbelievable hardship and danger. La Salle and his party of five men battled ice in the rivers as they paddled their canoes northeastward in early spring. They donned snowshoes to drag the canoes around icy obstacles. When the ice jams became too bad, they abandoned the canoes and continued on foot. They were short of food; only La Salle escaped falling ill. Faced by flood-swollen rivers, they built rafts to cross them. On they walked, through mud and slush, part of the time through hostile Indian country, until they reached Fort

Miami. Pausing only briefly, they kept plodding across Michigan until they reached the site of Detroit. On Lake Erie they built birchbark canoes and kept going. After sixty-five days and a trip of a thousand miles, La Salle reached Fort Frontenac in Canada. His arrival at his destination should have been a moment of happiness, but more bad news awaited him. The ship bringing a cargo of trading goods from France had been wrecked at the mouth of the St. Lawrence River!

Life seemed to be loaded against La Salle. But he wouldn't quit. He made his way back to Illinois, assembled a party of Frenchmen and Indians, and led a canoe caravan all the way down the Mississippi to the Gulf of Mexico.

After three years of hardships, perils, and disappointments that would have crushed most men, La Salle on April 9, 1682, planted a cross at the mouth of the Mississippi and proclaimed the land Louisiana, in honor of the King of France.

"*Vive le Roi!*" shouted the party. A volley of musket shots shook the air. "*Vive le Roi!*"

La Salle had achieved one part of his dream; he had linked the Great Lakes with the Gulf of Mexico under the rule of his faraway king. But tragedy still stalked him. He returned to France, outfitted a new expedition, and brought a force of men by ship through the Caribbean to establish a post at the mouth of the Mississippi. Missing their goal, they landed in Texas. There they fell into such troubles that the men revolted. La Salle set out on another desperate forced march to his home territory, the Great Lakes, but this time his luck had run out. Three mutinous men shot him to death in Texas territory on March 19, 1687.

Through the efforts of this tireless explorer, arrogant and demanding but far-sighted and determined, the Great Lakes were to stay under French rule for nearly three-quarters of a century.

Then, in one of history's most famous, if brief, battles, control of the lakes passed from French to British hands when the Redcoats led by General James Wolfe scaled the heights of Quebec at night and defeated the French under General Louis Montcalm.

In the summer of 1759 a large British fleet sailed up the St.

La Salle's explorations took him into a wilderness world far different from his native France, where he was a man of social distinction and political influence.

Lawrence to Quebec. That historic city lies on the north bank of the wide river, partly on a low, narrow plain at water level, and partly atop the spectacular rocky cliff. Montcalm kept most of his defending force of French soldiers and Canadian militiamen on the cliffs and in defensive positions downstream. All summer the British cannons hurled iron balls across the river from Port Levis into the stone houses of the lower town and the walled fortress high above it. The defenders stood fast. Recently workmen restoring old houses in the lower town as historical sites dug some of these cannon balls from the walls in which they had been imbedded for more than two hundred years, plastered over for much of that time.

September came, with hints of approaching winter. Wolfe still had not found a way to get his troops up the rock. One day while scanning the cliffs through his spyglass from the other shore he watched women doing their laundry at the river's edge. On the cliff above them he saw clothes spread out to dry.

"There must be a path there," he thought. "If women carrying bundles of clothes can go up, my soldiers can, too."

Early on September 13 a band of twenty-four British soldiers climbed the path, silenced the few defenders at the top, and summoned other men to follow. In the morning Montcalm was amazed to find the entire red-coated British army drawn up on the Plains of Abraham. In the battle that followed the British defeated the surprised French garrison. Both Wolfe and Montcalm died of wounds while leading their men.

For the British, possession of Quebec was like putting a plug in a bottle. The French inland around the Great Lakes were cut off. Soon the British had control of French Canada and ownership of all the Great Lakes. They were not to keep the lakes unchallenged for long, however. Barely a quarter-century later the American colonists along the Atlantic Coast won their independence in the Revolutionary War and forced the British permanently back into Canada, north of the Great Lakes.

5

Mighty Mac and the Turtle

Driving up the slopes of Mighty Mac when the fog hangs over the Straits of Mackinac gives a motorist an eerie feeling. Lonely and isolated, he soars higher and higher into the sky. Nothing is visible except a steel-bordered concrete path ahead, disappearing a few yards farther on into the gray mass. Far below, a whistle bellows mournfully—a cargo ship loaded with iron ore feeling its way between the spans of the world's longest suspension bridge.

As the northbound motorist nears the top of the arching structure, the fog breaks. Below is spread one of the most historic scenes in North America. To the left, Lake Michigan. To the right, joined by the strait, Lake Huron. In the right foreground a few miles distant, the island the Indians called Michilimackinac, the Great Turtle, and today's tourists call Mackinac Island. It is pronounced Mackin-aw. Ahead at the northern end of the bridge is St. Ignace, where Pére Marquette is buried. And behind, at the southern foot of the bridge, is the reconstruction of Fort Mackinac, where two hundred years ago Chippewa Indians carried out one of the bloodiest massacres of frontier history.

It is a fragile moment snatched unexpectedly from time. The motorist has a bird's-eye view of 350 years of history during which

The Mackinac Bridge joins the lower and upper peninsulas of Michigan. Beneath it pass a procession of lake cargo boats and foreign ships traveling between Lake Michigan and the other Great Lakes.

the French, the British, and the Americans contended for control of the strategic spot whose ownership means control of the Great Lakes water highway.

The bridge itself is an engineering marvel. The Straits of Mackinac, approximately five miles wide at the narrowest point and nearly three hundred feet deep, not only provide the water link between Lake Michigan and Lake Huron but separate the Lower and Upper Peninsulas of Michigan. Until the bridge was built in the 1950's the straits were a formidable barrier between the two parts of the state. The Indians made the crossing by canoe. In more modern times, ferryboats plied between Mackinaw City at the tip of the Lower Peninsula to St. Ignace on the Upper. But in winter the straits freeze solid, to the depth of two or three feet, halting such traffic.

Far back in 1884 the people of Michigan first talked about bridging the straits. The idea didn't become a reality for another seventy years because of the engineering difficulty and the great cost. Known affectionately as Mighty Mac, the span was opened

Each Labor Day morning the Mackinac Bridge is closed to automobile traffic and thousands of persons hike the five-mile length of the span.

November 1, 1957. To celebrate its existence, on Labor Day morning each year the bridge is closed to automobile traffic and thousands of persons hike across its five-mile span in the Annual Mackinac Bridge Walk. The governor of Michigan often leads the procession.

At the center of Mighty Mac's main span, the highway is 199 feet above the water. Large ships pass under it with room to spare. The two main towers to which the suspension cables are attached rise 552 feet above the water and are anchored on bedrock 210 feet below the surface. Engineers have calculated that there are 42,000 miles of wire in the main cables supporting the bridge, spun laboriously and often at great peril by crews suspended high above the water, buffeted by the winds that sweep through the straits.

No such bridge was in the dreams of the explorers, fur traders, priests, and soldiers who made Mackinac a wilderness outpost of crucial importance. Their concern was with surviving in the primitive surroundings and upholding the glory of the flags that flew by turn over the straits. The fleur de lis of France was first, then the British Union Jack, and finally the Stars and Stripes. Before them all, of course, were the Indians.

The first French explorers from Quebec reached the straits in 1634, when Nicolet claimed the island for the king of France. A French missionary priest established a mission for the Indians there in 1670. The island became a gathering place for trappers, soldiers, and *voyageurs*, as it had been for the Indians. In the early 1700's the French army, wanting to keep close watch on all the canoe traffic moving through the straits, built a fort on the tip of the Lower Peninsula, on the south shore across the strip of water from Mackinac Island. This they named Fort Michilimackinac.

Here a lively trade developed with the Indians. The natives came out of the forests carrying mink, muskrat, and beaver pelts which they traded to the French for colored beads, brandy, and fish hooks. Traders built homes within the log stockade of the fort. The Indians camped outside, coming and going casually through the fort's gates.

Eventually the effects of the fall of faraway Quebec to the British were felt at Michilimackinac. All the land in North America that had been French now belonged to the British, whose redcoated soldiers took possession of the fort in 1761.

The Indians, who had been trading with the French in friendly manner, did not like their new masters. They watched glumly as the Red Ensign was run up the flagpole, English replaced French

Residents of Mackinaw City reenact the massacre of Fort Michilimackinac on Memorial Day each year. Here participants and spectators are gathered outside the log walls of the reconstructed fort.

as the language spoken, and the fort was enlarged to make room for more soldiers. Several French Canadian trader families continued to reside inside the twenty-foot log walls, however. Canoes hauling cargo to and from Montreal arrived at the small dock outside the waterside gate in the walls.

Unsuspected by the British, the Indians led by their warrior chief Pontiac plotted an uprising against the frontier forts, especially Detroit and Mackinac, hoping with one coordinated blow to drive the hated conquerors from control of the western Great Lakes.

On the sultry morning of June 2, 1763, the Chippewas and the Sauks, friendly rival tribes, gathered outside Fort Michilimackinac to play *baggatiway*, an ancient Indian game that the French had adapted and called lacrosse. Each player had a long stick with a net at one end, with which he tried to hurl a ball past the other side's goal post. The Indians told the English officers and soldiers who gathered to watch that they were playing for a high wager.

The game progressed with shouting and shoving as the players chased the ball with sticks swinging. Finally the ball sailed high over the wall into the fort. The players rushed in a mass through the gate to retrieve it. At that moment two Indians seized the fort commander, Captain George Etherington, and another officer. The squaws who had gathered around the gate to watch the game threw back their blankets, revealing tomahawks and knives. Grabbing the weapons, the warriors attacked the unsuspecting soldiers inside the fort.

Before they had time to reach their guns, seventy of the soldiers were hacked to death. The frenzied Indians dipped their hands in the victims' blood and smeared themselves with it. Yet amid the horror the French traders and their families were left untouched. They looked on as the Indians, shouting war cries, held the soldiers between their knees and scalped them with their tomahawks.

Alexander Henry, a young English trader living at the fort, had not gone outside to watch the ball game because a canoe was leaving for Montreal the next day and he was writing letters to send on it. At the sound of anguished shrieks, Henry looked out the window and saw the attack in progress. He realized that soon the Indians would reach him, too.

From his house it was a few feet to the log home of his next-door neighbor, a Frenchman, M. Charles Langlade. Henry ran across into the other house and cried, "Hide me, please!"

Langlade shrugged his shoulders, said "No," and turned away.

Taking pity on Henry's desperate circumstances, a Pawnee Indian woman slave in the Langlade household beckoned him to follow her. She showed him the steps up to the garret through a door, which she locked behind him. Henry found himself in a windowless attic separated from the lower story only by loosely laid planks, through which he could hear what was happening below.

Moments later four Indians came into the house, asking whether any Englishman was hiding there.

"I do not know of any," Langlade replied truthfully, because he was not aware that the Indian woman had concealed Henry. "Look for yourselves."

Frantically Henry scrambled into a corner of the garret behind a pile of birchbark buckets used in making maple sugar, not much of a screen but all there was. He watched the garret door open. In the light reflected from below he saw four Indians enter the room. Their almost naked bodies were painted with blood. Each held a dripping tomahawk.

The Indians peered around the room, so close to Henry that he could have touched one of them. But the young Englishman's clothing was dark and so was the garret. The Indians failed to see him. To his immense relief they returned downstairs.

Although safe for the moment, Henry realized how critical his plight was. With the Indians in command of the fort, he saw no way to escape even if he could sneak out of the Langlade home. His worry grew greater a few hours later when Madame Langlade came to the attic on an errand and found him. She brought him water to drink and agreed to let him hide through the night.

Not long after sunrise the Indians returned to the Langlade home, drunk from an all-night carouse with the fort's liquor supply.

"We have not found the English trader's body. He must still be hiding," one of them said.

Listening through the boards, Henry was terrified to hear Madame Langlade say to her husband in French, "We must turn him over to them. If we don't they may take revenge against our children. It is better for him to die, than them."

Her husband agreed. He explained to the Indians that Henry had been hidden in the garret without his knowledge and that they were free to take him.

Hearing what appeared to be his death sentence, Henry decided to die bravely. He stood in full view of the Indians as they entered the upper room. Their appearance was frightening. One of them, Wenniway, was an acquaintance of Henry's. His entire body was smeared with charcoal and grease, even his face, except for a white spot two inches in diameter around each eye.

Wenniway grabbed the Englishman by the collar of his coat and, staring at him, placed the point of his knife at the captive's breast. Seconds passed. Henry tensed, waiting for the knife to plunge in. Then, in one of those strange whims that characterized Indian behavior, Wenniway dropped his arm and said, "I won't kill you!"

For Henry, it was as though a miracle had happened to stay the hand of the intoxicated Indian. "I have been in many wars against the Englishmen and have taken many scalps," Wenniway explained. "But I have lost a brother in one war. His name was Musinigon. I shall call you after him."

What happened to Henry after this reprieve was, in his own later words, more like a dream than reality. During the next several days his circumstances changed repeatedly; at one moment he appeared safe, then he was thrown into jeopardy again, only to be saved once more.

He was left temporarily in the garret by Wenniway, but was taken away later by an Indian who said Wenniway had sent him.

This was a man who owed Henry money from trading transactions. Outside the house, the Indian forced the Englishman to trade clothing with him, then marched him away from the fort into the sand dunes along the shore. Henry realized that the man intended to kill him. As the Indian plunged his knife at Henry, the trader struck his assailant's arm, knocked him down, and ran back to the fort. There he was confined with nineteen other English officers, soldiers, and civilians, including Captain Etherington, the commandant, who inexplicably had been taken captive by the Indians rather than being killed as the rest of the garrison were.

The next day was the third of their ordeal. Henry and the others were placed in canoes and forced to paddle out into Lake Michigan toward Beaver Island, forty-five miles away. They were told that they were to be killed and eaten. A Mackinac fog covered the water and they had to paddle close to shore. When they reached Fox Point, eighteen miles to the west, Indians on shore beckoned the party to land. As the canoes neared the beach, a hundred shouting Indians splashed out into the water and dragged the prisoners from their canoes onto the land.

It appeared that the prisoners were about to be put to death. But another weird twist in their story developed. Their new captors were Ottawas who were angry with the Chippewas because they had not been consulted in advance about the fort massacre. So they seized the Chippewas' prisoners in revenge.

"We are your friends," the Ottawas told the Englishmen. Yet that same night they took their captives back to Fort Michilimackinac and, after a council of peace between the Indian tribes, turned the Englishmen back to the Chippewas. By then Henry and his companions were totally baffled by the unpredictable ways of the Indians.

The next morning the captives were led before the Chippewa warriors and their chief in a council lodge. Their fate was to be decided, again. Henry was surprised and pleased to see his longtime Chippewa friend and self-proclaimed "brother," Wawatam, enter the lodge with his family, carrying a load of merchandise. This he placed at the feet of the war chief.

Wawatam had not been seen during the days of the massacre. He had, in fact, been ordered to leave the area by the war chief to prevent him from telling the attack plans to his white friend. Now Wawatam sought to make amends.

He told the chief and his fellow braves, "I bring these goods to buy off every claim which any man among you may have on my brother, as his prisoner."

The warriors filled their pipes and smoked in silence. The war chief arose and spoke. "We accept your present; and you may take him home with you."

Thus it was that Alexander Henry's life was saved, although seven other Englishmen were put to death as a result of the decisions made in the council lodge after Wawatam led him out.

After word arrived that the other parts of Pontiac's conspiracy had failed, including the intended capture of Detroit, the Indians at Fort Michilimackinac paddled across the straits to Mackinac Island in the belief that it would be safer from an English counterattack. English troops reoccupied the fort. Eventually in 1781 they too moved over to Mackinac Island into a new fort built high on a bluff overlooking the harbor. This fort passed into American hands after the Revolutionary War, and in the 1800's the island was the headquarters of John Jacob Astor's fur trade. The English recaptured it for a time during the War of 1812.

Visitors to Mackinac Island today step into a different kind of world. No automobiles! Transportation on the summer-resort island is restricted to horse-drawn vehicles and bicycles. Three miles long and two miles wide, rising to a high point in the middle, the island is said to have reminded the Indians of a turtle, which is how it acquired the name Michilimackinac. On summer days thousands of visitors cross the straits from Mackinaw City in a half-hour ferryboat ride. As they step ashore they see horse-drawn wagons rolling slowly through the streets of the white frame village tucked beneath the old fort. They can visit the fort and look out through the gun ports of the stone blockhouses commanding the harbor. Each week during the summer an honor Boy Scout troop from Michigan mounts guard at the fort, per-

Automobiles are forbidden on Mackinac Island, so traffic consists of horse-drawn vehicles and bicycles. Old Fort Mackinac stands on the bluff above the village.

Summer visitors to Mackinac Island cycle through the village beneath the walls of Fort Mackinac. Guns mounted on the walls once pointed out across the Straits of Mackinac.

The Grand Hotel on Mackinac Island is the world's largest summer hotel. Standing on a high point above the Straits of Mackinac, it is a luxurious reminder of days when such hotels were favorite vacation destinations around the Great Lakes.

forming some of the same duties that the British Redcoats and the early American soldiers once did—plus posing for photographers.

Near the fort on another high point above the harbor is the renowned Grand Hotel, the world's largest summer hotel, a gleaming white structure whose porch extends its entire 800-foot length. The Grand Hotel with its rolling green gardens and scenic vista across the straits still operates in the grand style of the resort hotels that dotted the Great Lakes shores three-quarters of a century ago.

When the seasons change and bitter winter closes in, life on Mackinac Island alters. The straits freeze solid to a depth of almost three feet, all shipping stops, and the four hundred year-around residents settle down for quiet months of isolated existence. The hotels and fort are closed. The residents lay in food and fuel supplies to carry them through until spring. Snowmobiles cross the ice from the mainland occasionally. In the snow and silence, it is easy to sense a kinship with the Indians, the missionaries, the soldiers and fur traders for whom the island was the center of life for so long.

Fort Michilimackinac on the mainland was abandoned when the island fort was built. Swept by winds, snow, and sand, the log structures disintegrated until only a few remnants were left. In recent years with the help of old maps and archeological excavations the fort has been rebuilt into an authentic replica. Visitors can see it almost as it was the day the Indians traded their lacrosse sticks for tomahawks. Each Memorial Day the residents of the community reenact the massacre that left such a trail of blood across Great Lakes history.

Although Beaver Island did not become the death place of Alexander Henry and his fellow prisoners, as the Chippewas had intended, the fourteen-mile-long island in upper Lake Michigan later became the scene of another strange and fatal episode. For a time it was under the rule of "King" James Strang, who formed a Mormon colony on the island in 1847.

Strang claimed a revelation that he was to serve as God's viceregent on earth and king of the colony he established on the remote forested island thirty-two miles out in the lake. Enough families believed him to build a colony of several hundred people. This stood at St. James, at the northern end of the island in a sheltered cove they called Paradise Bay. On July 8, 1850, the eccentric but dynamic Strang, wearing a bright red robe, had himself crowned King of the Earth. Four hundred followers promised to obey the laws he announced. One of these was the practice of multiple marriages.

Soon Strang's followers forced the non-Mormon inhabitants of the island to flee to the mainland. Tales of what was happening on the island angered the people at Charlevoix, the nearest community on the Michigan mainland shore. These stories were carried by disgruntled colonists who had come to dislike King Strang's

In winter the Straits of Mackinac freeze solid, halting ship traffic, and the Mackinac Bridge soars above a jumbled sheet of ice.

autocratic rule. When a group of fifteen of his followers came to the mainland in two open boats in 1853, mainlanders opened fire on them from a bluff. Six of the Mormons were wounded. Gathering up their casualties, the two boatloads started back across the open water for Beaver Island, pursued by three boats of mainland fishermen. Several miles out in the lake the pursuers drew close enough to fire their guns at the fleeing Mormons. Just as it seemed that all the Mormons would be shot, a ship sailing up Lake Michigan from Chicago to Buffalo happened to come along and took them aboard. Frustrated, the fishermen turned for home.

There was hatred for Strang on the island, too. Some of his followers decided that he had become too powerful and must be destroyed. Their plot was successful. But it destroyed the entire colony in the process.

On a June day in 1855 the United States revenue cutter *Michigan* tied up at the St. James pier. Her captain sent an officer ashore with a message to King Strang, "Please come aboard. I wish to talk with you."

As Strang approached the pier in response to the summons, two of his disgruntled followers stepped from a nearby store and shot him four times. They rushed aboard the boat and were given sanctuary. Strang's supporters demanded in vain that the murderers be put ashore, but instead the captain sailed them to Mackinac, where he let them go free. Thus made leaderless, the Mormon colony soon was driven from the island for good.

Its history of violence long in the past, today Beaver Island is a heavily wooded vacation spot for hunters and fishermen. It is reached during the summer by a twice-daily ferryboat from Charlevoix but is frozen in during the winter, one of those out-of-the-way places around the Great Lakes where the giant cities that ring the shores seem to belong to another, faraway world.

6

Perry Saves the Day

The international boundary between the United States and Canada is an imaginary line drawn by mapmakers down the middle of four Great Lakes and through the center of the four bottlenecks of the lakes system at Niagara, Detroit, Mackinac, and Sault Ste. Marie. It is so peaceful that only a few customs officers on both sides of the line guard it. There are no forts, no garrisons of troops. Every day tens of thousands of Americans and Canadians cross in both directions for business and pleasure. This frontier has been called a blue-water boundary because it runs through water the entire length of the lakes. The dividing line was established in 1783 by the Treaty of Paris that brought formal peace between the newly independent United States and Great Britain after the Revolutionary War.

It is a friendly frontier now; there is none friendlier anywhere in the world. It was not always so.

Although the British conceded all the land south of the Great Lakes and west to the Mississippi River to the young United States, their troops were slow to leave the forts they controlled in the wilderness west of the Appalachian Mountains. The victorious thirteen colonies were so busy getting themselves organized as a nation that they didn't have the time or the soldiers to drive the British from these outposts. So the Redcoats stayed on the American side of the lakes, profiting from the fur trade, until pushed out shortly before 1800. Disagreements between the new country and its former master continued. Formal war was declared between them again in 1812.

This War of 1812 went badly for the United States. British troops invaded Washington and burned the White House. Others crossed from Canada and captured Detroit, then repulsed American attempts to recapture it. This brought about the only naval battle ever fought on the Great Lakes, between the British and United States navies.

Both sides realized that since the boundary ran through the middle of the Great Lakes, naval control of those bodies of water could decide the war. Lake Erie was the critical place. The Americans controlled its eastern end, at Niagara, and the British the western end, at Detroit.

In these days of giant aircraft carriers and nuclear submarines that fire missiles from underseas, we find it difficult to visualize the kind of naval battles fought in those days. The warships were sailing vessels of wood, and they often battered each other with deadly broadsides of cannon balls from only a few hundred feet. Men of great bravery were needed.

To Lieutenant Oliver Hazard Perry fell the assignment of clearing the British warships from Lake Erie. Just twenty-seven years old, he faced an almost insurmountable assignment when he arrived to take command at Erie, Pennsylvania, a tiny port near the eastern end of Lake Erie. He had the authority but no warships. None could be brought from the Atlantic Ocean past Niagara Falls, so a fleet must be built on the lake.

For months gangs of shipbuilders cut down oak trees from the surrounding forests, hewed out planks, and shaped them into warships. Rigging and sails were attached to the tall masts. Cannon were fixed into positions on deck behind portholes in the wooden sides. While Perry urged on the construction crews, he kept a wary eye on the British ships on the lake, fearing an attack on his

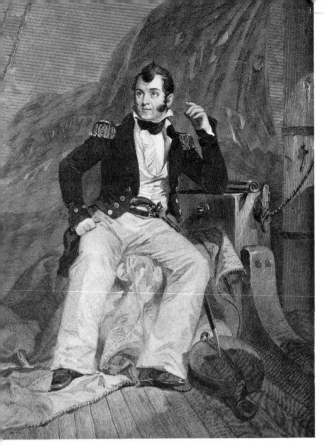

Oliver Hazard Perry, who defeated the British in a naval battle on Lake Erie during the War of 1812, posed for this painting in the U.S. Navy uniform of the period.

shipyard. He scrounged everywhere to find crews for the ships, since few experienced sailors were available. Part of the approximately five hundred sailors who manned Perry's fleet were soldiers borrowed from the United States Army under General William Henry Harrison. The general's force was assembled near the western end of Lake Erie, ready to advance on Detroit if Perry could drive the British fleet from the lake. Among the soldiers drafted as seamen were sharpshooting frontier riflemen from Kentucky.

At last, in August, 1813, Perry sailed his fleet out onto the blue waters and went to hunt the British. His two biggest warships, the *Lawrence* and the *Niagara*, were of about five hundred tons each, less than a tenth the size of an ordinary Great Lakes cargo ship today.

At dawn on September 10 the nine ships of the American fleet were anchored in Put-In Bay, a small, sheltered island near the western end of the lake. Known officially as South Bass Island, one of a small island group, Put-In Bay lies a few miles out in the lake from Sandusky, Ohio.

A lookout at the masthead shouted, "Sail ho!"

Boatswains' pipes shrilled, the sailors hurried on deck to their posts. A signal was made by Perry from his flagship, the *Lawrence*, "Enemy in sight! Get under way!"

As the American fleet sailed out of Put-In Bay, the British fleet of six warships advanced south toward them from the Detroit area under command of Captain Robert Heriot Barclay, a veteran deep-sea fighter. The spreading canvas sails of the opposing fleets glistened in the brilliant morning sunshine as they neared each other.

Perry had more ships. The British were more experienced, however; their ships were bigger and better tested, and they had the advantage of long-range firepower. Their guns could shoot farther than the Americans' could, enabling Barclay to strike the first blow.

"We must sail in and engage them at close range," Perry told his captains as they planned their tactics. "At short distance our guns are better than theirs."

The wind was from the southwest, unfavorable to the American vessels. They had difficulty sailing around the sheltering islands into position to meet the oncoming British, who had the wind advantage for maneuvering. At times Perry's ships made only enough headway to sail forward at less than three miles an hour, which is hardly plunging into battle at a breakneck pace.

Unexpectedly the wind shifted to the southeast. The Americans' sails filled and the tactical advantage shifted to them. Sailors spread sand on the decks and soaked it with water, to give them better footing when the blood of the wounded men splattered, a grim precaution often used in the sea warfare of those days. At the guns, men stood stripped to the waist with handkerchiefs bound around their foreheads.

Perry unfolded a large blue flag with the brave command, "Don't give up the ship!" Three lusty cheers rose from the crew of

75

the *Lawrence* as the flag was hauled up to the ship's fore-royal. Crewmen on the other American vessels sailing close behind repeated the shouts.

Drums and fifes on the flagship called the men to their battle stations with the strident air, "All hands, all hands, all hands to quarters!" Tense silence prevailed as the opposing fleets drew near. When the gap had closed to a mile, a cannon ball from the British flagship *Detroit* splashed into the water short of the *Lawrence*. Another followed, and another, striking home at their target. Splinters of wood rattled across the deck, and in the rigging above gaping holes appeared. The lake waters were pockmarked with spray from ill-aimed cannon balls.

"Sail closer!" Perry commanded. The signal was sent from ship to ship by trumpet blasts. The battle was joined, each ship concentrating its fire on a chosen vessel in the enemy fleet. Smoke swirled around the decks. The roar of the cannon broadsides made shouts inaudible for more than ten feet. Around the deck of the *Lawrence* men fell, dead or wounded, from the British cannon fire and the flying debris.

Among those aboard the *Lawrence* in the heat of the battle was Alexander Perry, the commander's thirteen-year-old brother. His job was to deliver commands from his brother to the officers and men firing the guns and handling the sails. He ran from post to post, shouting his brother's orders over the screams of the wounded and the din of the cannonades.

Perry's dog, a black spaniel, had been placed in the crockery closet before the firing began. By chance one of the first enemy shots smashed into the closet, sending a shower of broken plates and cups clattering down on the terrified dog. It barked and howled constantly for the next three hours but miraculously came through the carnage unharmed.

Below deck the ship's surgeon, Usher Parsons, had set up a primitive hospital in a hold. Wounded men limped or were carried down from their guns for emergency treatment but even there were not safe. Five times during the battle cannon balls tore through the side of the ship into the hospital quarters, killing several men.

Perry's flagship still could not reach the *Detroit* with her short-range broadsides. She kept bearing in on the British vessel, suffering heavily from that ship's long guns. Since for some reason the second largest American vessel, the *Niagara*, failed to come up close as Perry had ordered, the *Lawrence* took the brunt of the combined assault from the *Detroit* and Barclay's second ranking ship, the *Queen Charlotte*.

At a distance of only three hundred yards, the broadsides from the opposing ships reached hideous intensity. Perry had sent several of the Kentucky soldiers high up into the rigging with their rifles. These backwoodsmen, who had never been on a ship before, let alone in a naval battle, had become deadly shots while hunting squirrels and other game. Now they put their skill to work as snipers. Bracing their legs around the ropes, they fired down from their precarious, swaying perches at the British sailors with devastating effect.

Outnumbered two to one, Perry's *Lawrence* was battered until she became only a derelict hulk. The enemy fire ripped her sails and rigging to shreds and smashed her rudder, so she could only drift. Blood flowed on her decks as the gunners fell at their posts, their faces blackened with powder. Perry himself fired the only remaining gun until it, too, was knocked out of action. Of the 103 men aboard fit for duty, 83 were killed or wounded. Rarely in a naval battle had a warship suffered such a pounding.

His ship was destroyed but Perry's determination was not. "If I can prevent it, the American flag will not be hauled down this day," he said. He did lower his banner that proclaimed, "Don't give up the ship," and with a few remaining able-bodied men dropped a rowboat into the water at the stern of the *Lawrence*. Thinking that the American flagship had surrendered, the British sailors set up a triumphant cheer. But too soon. The American flag still flew. By now the reluctant *Niagara* had sailed to within a half mile of Perry's stricken vessel. The commander and his men set

Under fire, Perry crosses to the *Niagara* from his stricken flagship *Lawrence* at the height of the battle.

out to row to her through the smoke that clung to the water. Perceiving his plan, the British concentrated their cannon and rifle fire on the rowboat. Perry stood resolutely in the stern while the men bent to their oars. Bullets punctured the rowboat's sides and shattered some of the oars. Splashes of water churned up by the cannon balls soaked the men. But Perry's luck held. Miraculously, the rowboat and its men reached the *Niagara*.

Once aboard this fresh vessel, which was still almost undamaged, Perry ran up his famous blue pennant and made her his flagship. One ship had been shot out from under him, but this was not enough to discourage him from close combat. He turned the bow of the *Niagara* straight for the enemy formation.

Perry held his fire until he was almost upon the three chief enemy vessels, the *Detroit*, *Queen Charlotte*, and *Lady Prevost*, grouped to meet him. Then Perry had another stroke of luck. An American ball shot away part of the *Queen Charlotte*'s sails and she collided with the *Detroit*. Their sails became entangled, holding them together. From a distance of only one hundred feet, Perry's guns raked the helpless British ships with broadside after broadside. Passing them, he opened fire on the *Lady Prevost*, and turning, laid broadsides into the approaching British brig *Hunter*. Back through the heart of the shattered British fleet Perry took the *Niagara* again, still firing.

A surviving officer on the deck of the *Queen Charlotte* tied a white handkerchief to a boarding pike and waved it. The first British ship had surrendered. Almost immediately the others followed. Their crews, too, had suffered extremely heavy casualties. Barclay, their commander, had been struck twice but had the doctor carry him back up on deck for the last critical moments. Fifteen minutes after Perry had climbed aboard the *Niagara*, the battle was over.

For all its viciousness, naval warfare of the early nineteenth century was conducted with formality and a gentlemanly concern for the courtesies.

Perry returned to the disabled *Lawrence* by rowboat to receive the formal surrender of the British. As he climbed aboard he asked, "Where is my brother?" The ship was searched, amid fears that Alexander had been blown overboard, until he was found in his bunk below. Exhausted from the battle, he had stretched out on his bed and fallen asleep.

Perry stood at attention in the blood-splattered wreckage on the *Lawrence*'s deck as the British officers, one from each ship, came aboard in full dress uniform. Each man ceremoniously extended his sword with its hilt toward the victorious commander. With a smile Perry refused them. "Keep your swords, sirs, they have been bravely used and worn." He sent an American officer to the *Detroit* to deliver his compliments to Barclay and to express sorrow that he had been wounded.

Then Perry wrote a note in pencil on the back of a dirty envelope, a message announcing the victory. He sent a man ashore in a rowboat to deliver it to General Harrison. His words were to become among the most famous in American military history: "We have met the enemy and they are ours; two ships, two brigs, one

This 352-foot monument at Put-In Bay on Lake Erie commemorates Perry's naval victory over the British fleet during the War of 1812.

schooner, and one sloop."

The elaborate gallantry between victor and vanquished went even further. Perry later went aboard the *Detroit* to visit Barclay and found in talking with the British officers that they were without money. Payroll funds had not been delivered to the outpost base at Detroit. So the victorious commander lent the enemy officers, now his prisoners, a thousand dollars! He and Barclay struck up a friendship that lasted the rest of Perry's life.

Both fleets limped back to Put-In Bay, where they drew up in line. The bodies of the American and British officers killed in the battle were buried side by side beneath a group of trees while Perry stood with his arm around the weakened Barclay.

Today a monument rises 352 feet above Put-In Bay, commemorating Perry's victory. It overlooks the burial ground of the officers, and the bay where the boats of summer vacationers form a pattern of white sails on blue waters. The memorial was built in 1913, the centennial of the naval battle, as a symbol of peace between Canada and the United States.

Put-In Bay and other islands in the group are served by one of the most unusual airlines in the United States. Its fleet consists of two Ford Tri-Motor planes built in the late 1920's, among the few

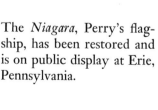

The *Niagara*, Perry's flagship, has been restored and is on public display at Erie, Pennsylvania.

such planes still in operation. These lumbering "Tin Gooses" fly at eighty-five miles an hour, take off in six hundred feet, and carry fifteen passengers along with groceries, laundry, hardware, and pets for the islanders.

After lying for years at the bottom of Misery Bay at Erie, the *Niagara* was brought up from its underwater grave and reconstructed. Timbers of the original keel are preserved in the rebuilt ship, and in other respects it has been restored as closely as possible to its original condition. The *Niagara* is anchored at the foot of State Street in Erie and is open to visitors.

Once Britain's fleet had been cleared from the Great Lakes, her soldiers were forced to evacuate Detroit and Harrison's American troops quickly occupied it. The road to the West for the American pioneers was open, at last. As the echoes of the cannon ball barrages of that sea battle died away, the friendship that links the United States and Canada began.

7

Through the Soo

The traffic light in the river was green. The iron arm barring entrance to the huge Poe Lock at Sault Ste. Marie, Michigan, rose like the gate at a railroad crossing. With a toot of its whistle, the little boat advanced cautiously into the thousand-foot long chamber and came to rest at the far end. Then, inching into the same lock, crept a mammoth iron ore boat riding high in the water in ballast. Ahead the steel gates, clamped shut, barred a wall of Lake Superior water from flooding into the lock. At the rear of the chamber the other pair of gates swung closed.

A passenger standing on the deck of the small boat near water level felt as though he was in the bottom of a mammoth well, with no way out.

Nothing was visible in the deep private world of the lock except the high walls of concrete rising on both sides, the steel gates blocking the ends, the water below, and the sky far above. At his back the rusty red bow of the ore carrier loomed above the small boat, a giant and a midget trapped in the same cavern.

"Look, we're rising!" a companion exclaimed.

Almost imperceptibly the boat began to go up. The water level rose on the crisscross pattern of the walls, a few feet every thirty seconds like a bathtub filling, except that the inrushing water was not coming down from above, as from a bathtub's faucet, but was being forced up into the chamber through invisible pipes beneath.

Suddenly the view changed. The passenger's eyes came parallel to the top of the lock walls, then above them. To his surprise numbers of spectators were watching from a platform only a few feet away, and close behind them automobile traffic filled a busy downtown street of Sault Ste. Marie. Now his boat was at the level of the open water ahead. The front gates swung wide. With another whistle blast the small craft sailed out of the lock under the International Bridge into Lake Superior at a water level twenty-one feet higher than when it entered the lock at the Lake Huron end a half hour earlier.

Day and night, around the clock, a parade of vessels makes the trip through the four American locks at the "Soo," as Sault Ste. Marie is nicknamed. Sault in French means "falls"; thus, literally translated, Sault Ste. Marie means the Falls of St. Mary. So many ships pass through, in fact, that these are the busiest locks in the world. More shipping travels through these concrete-lined strips of water every year than moved through the Panama Canal and the Suez Canal combined in the days before the Israeli-Egyptian War of 1967 forced the Suez to close. This is despite the fact that the Soo locks are frozen shut about one-third of the year, choked by a sheet of ice.

For a long time after the white men came to the Great Lakes, Lake Superior was the "closed lake," inaccessible to boats from outside because they could not navigate through the tumbling white froth of the St. Marys River rapids, the short bottleneck connecting Lakes Superior and Huron. A fortune in copper and an even greater, unsuspected fortune in iron ore waited to be extracted from the land around the lonely forested shores of Lake Superior. Some day, too, the lake would become the shipping point for mountains of wheat grown on the prairies of the northern United States and southern Canada.

All of that was in the future, however. To the Indians, Lake Superior was a place of legend. It was Gitchee Gumee, the shining blue sea water, home of the hero Hiawatha. Eventually these leg-

This view of a ship in a lock on the Welland Canal gives the impression of being at the bottom of a well.

An aerial view of the Sault Ste. Marie locks, looking downstream from the Lake Superior end. Canada is on the far left, the United States on the right, with the International Bridge stretching across the center. The St. Marys River rapids are visible to the left of the locks.

Portions of the Lake Superior shore look much as they did when only the Indians inhabited the area. This scene is of the Upper Falls of the Pigeon River in the Minnesota area of the north shore.

ends were gathered into a book by Henry Rowe Schoolcraft, the first Indian agent sent by the United States government to Sault Ste. Marie in the 1820's. Schoolcraft mingled with the Indians and married a half-Indian woman. In the depths of winter when the settlement at the Soo rapids was snowbound, he put these legends into a book. A copy reached Henry Wadsworth Longfellow far away in Massachusetts. Intrigued by the beliefs of the Chippewa Indians, the poet put them into verse form as the beloved epic poem, "The Song of Hiawatha." When we read of swift-footed Hiawatha and the wigwam of Nokomis, his grandmother, it is easy to visualize how primeval the forest and the deep cold lake were. Even today there are dark thickets and rocky shores where with a little imagination one is able to see again the campfires of Hiawatha and his fellow tribesmen.

Black-robed French priests established a mission at the Soo, and in 1670 Sieur de St. Lusson, representing King Louis XIV of France, gathered the Indians into a conclave there. Ceremoniously a cross was planted and the French banner was raised on a crude cedar pole. A round of musketry was fired, a sound never before heard there. With a grand sweep of his hand the French leader proclaimed his distant king to be ruler over the Great Lakes and all lands whose waters drained into them. Quite a claim it was, too; far bigger than those early Frenchmen could possibly have realized—nearly 300,000 square miles.

For more than three hundred years there have been settlements at the St. Marys rapids. First the French came, then the British. After the Revolutionary War the Americans took possession of the south bank while the British kept the north bank. That is how two friendly but unrelated cities bearing the same name, Sault Ste. Marie, grew up facing each other on the Michigan and Ontario shores, now joined by the soaring International Bridge. While the Michigan city gets more of the shipping, the larger Canadian city is an important steel and paper-manufacturing center.

Although less than a mile long, the rapids are a formidable barrier. Pouring over their rock-strewn bottom at great speed, the water drops twenty-one feet. Passage up through the rapids is impossible for vessels of any kind, but daredevil Indians in birch-

Passengers cling to their seats as boatmen steer canoes through the St. Marys River rapids in the early 1900's. Such trips are no longer made.

bark canoes occasionally shot the rapids downstream to show their manhood. Courageous visitors made the trip as passengers in the early days, exhilarated by the frantic seven-minute ride. The first white woman to make the trip, Mrs. Anna Jameson, wife of the attorney general of Upper Canada, did it in 1837. She crouched in the bottom of the canoe as the foam surged over her and the Indian paddler maneuvered the ten-foot canoe through gaps in the rocks barely two feet wide, twisting and turning the craft to avoid instant disaster. "Giddy, breathless, and delicious excitement," Mrs. Jameson called her wild trip. Because of man-made controls the flow of the rapids is much less now than it was in those days, when Indians stood in their canoes at the foot of the swift current and hauled in whitefish with hand nets.

When the Americans began to develop the copper mines on the south shore of Lake Superior in the 1840's, the need for boats on the lake became apparent. A few small vessels had been built along its shores but had to operate without navigational aids. They had neither charts nor depth soundings. To enter a landing place, a captain had to send men ahead in a rowboat to find a channel. The only way to get boats into the lake from outside was to drag them overland from the Lake Huron end of the rapids through the middle of the little settlement on the Michigan side. Schooners and small steamboats were hauled laboriously from lake to lake by this method, up the portage road on rollers and skids like houses being moved. Weeks of heavy labor were required to pull the larger vessels from one end of the portage to the other. Once these boats began operating on Lake Superior, carrying cargo from the mines and settlements at the far end of the lake to the Soo, it was necessary to unload them and transport their cargo by land to waiting vessels below the rapids.

No longer quite closed to the outer world, Lake Superior still was almost isolated behind the Soo. A way to sail ships around the rapids must be found. Across the river the Canadians had built a small bypass canal with locks in 1797, so small that it could handle a vessel only about the size of a modern lifeboat. During the War of 1812, American soldiers crossed the river and smashed the locks, ending the experiment. But the idea of a canal was kept alive by those who dreamed of the day when shipping could sail out from Lake Superior to the world.

Back East in Washington, the advocates of a canal sought to interest the Congress in building it. But powerful men in Congress, like Henry Clay, saw no sense in spending money on such a project in the distant forests where only a few copper-mining speculators, traders, half-breeds, and Indians lived.

"It is beyond the remotest settlement in the United States, if not in the moon," Clay sneered.

Finally, in 1852, Congress voted to give the State of Michigan a subsidy of 750,000 acres of federal land if Michigan would build the canal. The members thought that this was much cheaper than appropriating money. There were millions of empty acres out there that nobody wanted, anyway.

About the time Congress acted, a young traveling salesman named Charles T. Harvey arrived in Sault Ste. Marie. His business was selling Fairbanks scales to the merchants and miners. At twenty-three Harvey was a shrewd Yankee trader with an eye for opportunities that might develop in the raw wilderness that was his sales territory. Unfortunately, the first thing he acquired at the Soo was a case of typhoid fever.

As he recuperated from his illness, he watched the horse-drawn portage tram cars trundling cargo around the rapids on wooden rails, and boats being hauled up the street. The possibilities of a canal excited him. He wrote urgent letters back to the Fairbanks Company headquarters in Vermont, urging it to undertake the building of the canal. "A three quarter mile canal here not costing over $400,000 would enable any lake craft to load at Buffalo and go through to Fond du Lac (end of the lake) 600 miles west of here . . ." he explained.

His employers were financial plungers, as well as builders of precision scales. They were stirred by the idea of building such a canal a thousand miles away in the wilderness. The Fairbanks brothers enlisted the help of other eastern financiers, formed the St. Marys Falls Ship Canal Company, won the construction contract from the State of Michigan, and appointed Harvey to supervise the job.

Building the canal proved to be far trickier business than selling scales to store owners. Harvey was a hard worker but had no

Naval parade through the Soo locks in 1905, sailing toward Lake Superior. The picture shows the types of passenger and cargo ships then in common use on the Great Lakes.

Ships of U.S. Steel Corporation's Great Lakes Fleet rendezvous at the Duluth, Mesabe & Iron Range Railway ore docks in Duluth after leaving their winter berths. Six gravity-fed ore docks in Duluth-Superior, largest of their kind in the world, load about 35 million tons of cargo into approximately 2000 ships during a shipping season.

training as an engineer. He made mistakes. Getting and keeping gangs of diggers at the remote location was difficult. Repairs for the tools were hard to make. Work almost halted during the heavy winter months. Stone brought in to line the lock walls was porous and wouldn't hold the water. The lock gates had to be made in Detroit and shipped in. Harvey's estimated $400,000 cost was exceeded with the job barely half done.

Despite the difficulties, the tandem locks, each lifting or lowering a vessel nine feet, went into operation on June 18, 1855, and the *Illinois*, a wooden, wood-burning steamer, made the passage up from Lake Huron to Lake Superior. At last the "closed" lake was open to the world, at a cost of almost $1,000,000.

By later standards the first locks were small and primitive, but they were large enough to handle any boat sailing the Great Lakes in those days just before the Civil War. As the ships grew, so did the locks. New chambers, deeper and longer, replaced the original ones and were in turn replaced as the needs grew. Electric gates replaced the hand-cranked ones.

A visitor to the Soo today sees four American locks of varying

Three ore carriers attempt passage through a five-mile field of wind-rowed ice in Lake Superior shortly after clearing Duluth on their first trips of a new navigation season. Standing by in the background is the Duluth-based Coast Guard cutter *Woodrush*.

lengths and depths, side by side. Ships can be raised in some of them while others are being lowered simultaneously a few feet away. The process goes on ceaselessly except during the three or four months when the river freezes solid; then the locks are drained and repairs made to their machinery.

Early in April the action begins again when an icebreaker plows a path through the melting white barricade for the first of the waiting ships. Depending upon when the big freeze-up hits—it can come very quickly—ships sometimes are locked solidly into the river ice for months until the thaw comes. The crews can walk ashore.

Largest of the four American locks is the Poe Lock, completed in 1968, capable of handling a ship 1000 feet long and 105 feet wide. The other locks—the MacArthur, Davis, and Sabin—handle ships of lesser depth. The locks are operated by the United States Army Corps of Engineers. Each year approximately seventeen

Accumulated drift ice from Lake Superior crowds the surface of a
Soo lock as a ship makes the downward passage late in the season. Two
other vessels, upward bound to Lake Superior, are in a lock to the
right, and others await their turns in the background.

A heavily loaded cargo vessel leaves a Soo lock at the Lake Huron end
after being lowered from the Lake Superior level.

thousand ships pass through them, free of charge.

Across the international boundary, on the other side of the St. Marys River, the Canadian government operates one lock, older and smaller than the American ones. This is used mostly by small boats and pleasure craft.

Lake Superior beyond the locks was likened by the Indians in their imagination to a bow and arrow—the straight south shore forms the string, the long arching north shore the bow, and the Keeweenaw Peninsula sticking out toward midlake from the south shore the arrow.

Before the canal, most cargoes shipped down to the Soo from the settlements along the south and northwest shores of the lake were furs and fish. The furs were gathered by agents of the Hudson's Bay Company and the rival American Fur Company headed by John Jacob Astor. Lake Superior was full of delicious whitefish, to the great joy of pioneer fishermen. At one time, between the French defeat at Quebec and the American victory in the Revolutionary War, the lake was entirely in British hands. They sought to enforce a trade monopoly. In 1765 Alexander Henry, who had miraculously escaped the Indian massacre at Fort Michilimackinac, was given exclusive trading rights for the entire Lake Superior area by the fort commander. Distances and the lack of transportation made this right less profitable than it sounds, but it was a lucrative gift nonetheless while it lasted.

The white explorers heard from the Indians about copper ore existing along the south shore and on Isle Royale, an island off the northwest shore. They found remnants of Indian diggings for copper. Even more exciting, they discovered chunks of pure copper on the surface. The glint of wealth came to their eyes. Specimens of the ore were shipped back East, causing excitement among mining speclators in the great cities of the United States and Europe. The copper mines that were developed in this boom were situated mostly on and near the Keeweenaw Peninsula.

Once the canal was opened and the shipment of copper became practical, a great rush developed. Copper mined there in the last half of the 1800's and shipped to the world through the Soo helped to build American cities and bring them electric light. Like so many of America's natural resources, however, the copper mines of Lake Superior have been almost exhausted. Little copper mining remains in the area.

While probing around for copper in the mid-1800's, mining men discovered iron along the southern shore. A party of miners on exploration in 1844 were puzzled because their magnetic compass whirled wildly. When they searched the ground they found chunks of iron ore of exceptional richness, a find whose value they didn't fully appreciate at first. They had their minds and hearts set on copper.

The first small quantity of iron ore was shipped out in 1846, being trundled down the portage at the Soo. The need for direct-through shipment of ore was a major economic pressure for building the canal. Gold hunters working inland from the northwest shore of the lake, in the eastern corner of Minnesota, discovered the most extensive iron ore deposit of all, the Mesabi Range. This range and other nearby areas are yielding hundreds of train carloads of ore a month. These are loaded aboard the ore ships at the twin ports of Duluth, Minnesota, and Superior, Wisconsin. Two-

The bulk carrier *D.G. Kerr* takes on a load of iron ore at the Duluth, Minnesota, docks for transportation to a steel mill on the lower lakes.

An open pit mine, source of the steel from which thousands of American buildings have been constructed. This is the Sherman mine at Chisholm, Minnesota.

thirds of the iron ore produced in the United States and Canada is shipped through the Soo Locks.

The type of ore being dug is different now from what it was thirty years ago. As the supply of rich ore was exhausted from deep shafts, surface mining for low grade ore called "taconite" was started. Ground to a fine powder, the ore is separated from the surrounding rock and formed into small pellets. These easily handled pellets, about the size of marbles, are shipped downlake to the steel mills.

Logging cut off much of the virgin forest around Lake Superior in the late 1800's and early 1900's; immense quantities of lumber moved through the canal until that resource, too, was almost exhausted. Heavy stands of new growth timber cover the land around the lake, however, and under careful control and replanting provide the raw material for the pulp paper mills.

Within recent years a paved highway has been built all around Lake Superior, a 1300-mile circular drive through forests and past rock formations, in areas where wild animals abound. At the extreme western end of the lake is the American lakehead, Duluth and Superior. Two hundred miles up the northwest shore from there is the Canadian lakehead, the city of Thunder Bay. This consists of the two long-time friendly rival neighboring cities of Fort William and Port Arthur, Ontario. Recently they combined legally into a single city, named Thunder Bay for the lake inlet on which both face. Through the huge grain elevators at this port, capable of storing more than one hundred million bushels, is funneled the output of the Canadian prairie wheatfields into the bulk carrier ships.

Were he to visit the earth, the legendary Hiawatha would marvel at what the white men have done along the shores of Gitchee Gumee. Still, on a dark night on Isle Royale, preserved as a primitive national park, or at remote points where the wind sighs in the trees and the lake waves beat against the rocks, he might feel the magic of ancient days when his moccasined feet sped through the forest in pursuit of the red deer.

8

The Great Cities Spring Up

A jet airliner taking off from O'Hare International Airport north-west of Chicago climbs quickly and circles above the towers of the second-largest American metropolis. Below on a sunny afternoon a passenger can see the thicket of skyscrapers along Michigan Boulevard. Beyond lies Lake Shore Drive—after that, the gleaming blue expanse of Lake Michigan dotted with pleasure boats. Out in the lake a heavily laden ship plows ahead with a cargo of iron ore from the distant shores of Lake Superior. This is going to the hungry steel furnaces of Gary, Indiana, whose flames shooting high into the sky flicker on the eastern horizon.

Chicago is called the Windy City. Anyone who has walked its streets on a winter day or watched a home-run ball lofted over the ivy-covered brick wall of Wrigley Field during a Chicago Cubs game knows why. Detroit is the Motor City, for equally obvious reasons. How amazed Antoine de la Mothe Cadillac, the aristocratic Frenchmen who built the first fortified settlement on the site of Detroit, would have been if he could have known that he would be remembered not for his bravery in facing the Indians but as the name of a luxurious automobile!

There is a sense of toughness, a flexing of sinews, in the names

The Chicago skyline provides the background for foreign ships docked at Navy Pier in Lake Michigan. These vessels have brought their cargoes through the St. Lawrence Seaway.

and nicknames of the great industrial cities that ring the shores of the Great Lakes. That's the kind of cities they are, aggressive and vigorous, grown from the wilderness, built with materials taken from the earth around the lakes. At first they were wooden towns, their lumber cut from the forests that once covered the land. Later they became cities of steel, made from the ore dug in the fabulously rich pits of the Upper Michigan Peninsula and Minnesota.

Great Lakes people are hardened by their climate. After the smiling months of summer have passed, they face harsh winters, especially those who live in the northern portion of Great Lakes country. Up in Green Bay, Wisconsin, capacity crowds have been

The first South African ship to visit Chicago, the *SA Transporter*, is docked at Navy Pier. The Chicago skyline rises in the background.

known to watch their Packers play professional football games when the temperature was ten below zero.

From the airliner window above Chicago, the passenger sees a metropolis stretching from the lake westward onto the prairie, bound together by the concrete threads of the expressway system. One hundred and fifty years ago the city had a population of fifty who lived in a few wooden homes around Fort Dearborn at the mouth of the Chicago River. Like Cleveland, Detroit, Milwaukee, Toledo, Buffalo, Toronto, and other cities on the lake shores, Chicago was a frontier outpost until a phenomenon happened. Millions of Europeans crossed the Atlantic Ocean to the New World during the 1800's. After landing at New York or Boston they pushed westward in search of a new life. They sought the abundant jobs that awaited them in the swiftly expanding inland cities, or the cheap farming land that lay beyond. The Great Lakes became a highway for one of the great migrations in history.

Many traveled by barge across New York State on the Erie

Scores of pleasure boats are tied up at protected docks in Bayview Park, Toledo, Ohio, ready for their owners to enjoy summertime sailing.

Buffalo, New York, is a major grain and shipping center, the destination of many vessels from Lake Superior carrying wheat grown in the fields of Canada.

Canal to Buffalo. There they boarded the paddle-wheel steamships for the West. Overcrowded at times to the danger point, their decks clogged with the possessions of the immigrants, these wooden vessels hauled the new arrivals to Cleveland, or Detroit, or all the way around to Chicago. Often the $7.00 steerage fare from Buffalo to Detroit took almost the last pennies of the newcomers, who often spoke no English.

When Charles Dickens came to the United States from England in 1842 to lecture in his role as a famous author, he made a trip on Lake Erie aboard one of these ships, the *Constitution*. Aware of the fire peril and the throbbing of the steam engines in the flimsy hull, he said he felt as though he had "lodgings on the first floor of a powder-mill." He was seasick, as were the other passengers. "It's almost as bad in that respect as the Atlantic," he complained.

As the immigrants of many nationalities and tongues flocked in, the cities grew. Factories created jobs. Soon the smoke from plant chimneys darkened the horizons of the new cities. Those sooty smoke clouds, which we abhor today for causing air pollution, were cheered by everyone then as a sign of prosperity.

Chicago had the most spectacular growth of all. Built on swampy land where the Chicago River flows into Lake Michigan, it expanded rapidly during the 1840's and 1850's, so fast that no provision had been made for proper sewers and drainage. The city council decided, "We must raise the entire downtown section out of the swamp." It ordered every building lifted four or five feet and new foundations added underneath. But life in Chicago was too busy to halt. Business went on as usual while hand-powered jacks were placed under the buildings and they were lifted into the air. A guest staying at the Tremont House wrote home, "I knew something was happening because the front stairs got progressively steeper each day." Other buildings were dragged on wooden skids to new locations by teams of horses. Their occupants watched from the windows or stood in the doorways puffing cigars while the houses went down the muddy streets.

On the windy evening of October 8, 1871, Chicago was a sprawling city of wooden buildings packed close together. Hardly anyone had built with brick; it was too slow and expensive. On the West Side of the city, where the Irish immigrants settled, Patrick O'Leary and his family lived in a shingled cottage. Behind the house in a barn where Mrs. O'Leary kept a cow, fire broke out that evening. Popular legend has it that the cow kicked over the kerosene lantern into the hay. Like a torch, the flames leapt to the next building. Soon they were beyond control. What followed was among the worst disasters in American history.

Blown by the wind, the billowing sheet of flame swept into the downtown area. Not only did it consume the buildings in its path but also the wooden sidewalks and even the streets themselves, which consisted of wooden blocks filled with pitch and creosote, laid like bricks. The flames jumped across the south branch of the Chicago River, west of downtown, and later across the main stream of the river to the North Side.

Seizing such valuables as they could carry, residents fled toward the lake front. Many took refuge in the water to escape the heat. One by one the city's best-known buildings erupted in balls of fire. Glass and metal melted in moments. An eyewitness reported, "The appearance was that of a vast ocean of flames, sweeping in mile-long billows and breakers over the doomed city. A square of substantial buildings would be submerged by it like a child's tiny heap of sand on the beach of a lake."

The fire burned for three days. When the last blackened embers had cooled and the damage could be counted, nearly 100,000 of the city's 300,000 people were homeless and almost four square miles in the heart of the city burned flat. How many were killed never was determined, but it was more than 250. Yet the day after the fire died out a fruit stand reopened in the rubble, starting the rebuilding process that was to make central Chicago emerge into its present lake-front skyline of steel and concrete and glass.

All the important cities on the Great Lakes have in common their location at or near the mouths of rivers emptying into the lakes. Many existed first as trading posts where the pioneer merchants built cabins in which they traded their goods, guns, and whiskey to the Indians for furs and corn. A river mouth was the logical location because the stream led to the interior country and the lake was the route over which the traders reached the outside world.

In most cases the cities grew in haphazard manner. Perhaps an informal lumbering business started in the forests behind the settlement. Additional settlers from the westward flow of immigrants stopped there for a few days, liked what they saw, and remained. Others followed, until a small city developed.

The birth of Cleveland, the industrial metropolis on the southern shore of Lake Erie, was somewhat different because it was planned.

After the Revolutionary War, a group of forty-nine Connecticut men purchased three million acres of land in the far-off Ohio country. One of their group, Moses Cleaveland, led a surveying party there in 1796 to establish a town where the Cuyahoga River twisted into the lake. Some distance upstream, they found, it was possible to make a portage to streams flowing south through Ohio to the Ohio River. This gave the city-to-be a connection to the Mississippi River which later generations developed into a busy canal.

Moses Cleaveland unloaded his surveying instruments and laid out the city, straddling the Cuyahoga. His party built a couple of cabins as a sign of good faith. A month later Cleaveland packed up and went back to his Connecticut home, never to visit the site again. Somehow the "a" was lost from the city he named after himself, but except for this mishap the city has grown just as he foresaw—and a thousand times as big.

Cleveland has developed as the eighth largest city in the United States on coal, steel, and ships. Iron ore is brought to its mills from Lake Superior. From inland, coal brought by train is either used in the city's mills or transshipped to steel mills elsewhere on the Great Lakes. Long ore ships maneuver up the winding Cuyahoga in a remarkable demonstration of piloting skill, a fascinating sight for those looking down from the upper floors of Cleveland's most famous landmark, the 52-story Terminal Tower. Sad to say, the river's waters long ago lost the clarity Moses Cleaveland knew.

Heavily polluted by oil, the Cuyahoga River burns at Cleveland, sending up billows of black smoke.

They are heavily polluted with oil and chemicals which turn them a horrible color. So much oil floats on the Cuyahoga's surface that it is called "the only river in the world to be proclaimed a fire hazard" because it actually has caught fire. When it did so in 1969, $100,000 damage was done to two bridges. This claim of exclusivity isn't quite true, however; the Buffalo River at the eastern end of Lake Erie also has been ignited several times.

Detroit, now the fifth largest city in the country, in its early days was a French town built around Fort Pontchartrain, which Cadillac established in 1701 to help hold the Great Lakes for the French king. The city's name originally was spelled d'étroit, which in French means "narrows," referring to the Detroit River,

The Ambassador Bridge spans the Detroit River between Detroit and Windsor, Ontario. Beneath it pass ships bound for ports on Lakes Huron, Michigan, and Superior.

connecting link between Lakes Huron and Erie. Among the city's streets are some with French names such as Beaubien, Dubois, and Rivard, commemorating pioneer landowning families.

Because the Detroit River winds, a strange quirk of geography has come about. At one point the United States is north of Canada! Most of Detroit's waterfront faces south while the shoreline of Windsor, Ontario, across the river, faces north. Through this channel under the soaring Ambassador Bridge that links Detroit and Windsor pass all the ships moving between the three upper lakes—Huron, Superior, and Michigan—and Lake Erie. It has been called the busiest stretch of waterway in the world, except in the winter months when most lake navigation ceases. From a military tactical standpoint, control of the Detroit River in war would be an essential goal, a fact that nobody even thinks about now because of the long friendship between the United States and Canada.

Ask almost anyone, "What do you think of when Detroit is mentioned?" and the answer is, "Automobiles." Truly, Detroit is the automotive capital of the world. Millions of automobiles and trucks are manufactured in and around the city. The giant automotive corporations, General Motors, Ford, and Chrysler, have their headquarters there. The decisions made by motor executives in Detroit determine what styles of automobiles people will be driving in many countries.

Although the automobile was not invented in Detroit, the city became a center for developing pioneer cars even before the start of the twentieth century. Mechanics worked in barns and backyard sheds, experimenting with ways to make a four-wheeled vehicle move with engine power developed from gasoline or electricity. Men were doing the same thing in other cities, but one by one their little companies quit business. The words Detroit and automobile became almost interchangeable. Partly this was due to the willingness of financiers in the city to lend money to the automakers, even in the days when many persons considered the primitive automobile a fad. They thought that it soon would be abandoned while the country would continue to depend upon the reliable old horse.

The individual who did most to make the automobile a household necessity was Henry Ford. He built his first crude two-cylinder car in a small back-yard machine shop during his spare hours away from his job with the Detroit Edison Company. That was in 1896. When he organized his own company in 1903 he had trouble raising money. One man whom Ford convinced to put up $2500 sold his stock sixteen years later for more than thirty million dollars after drawing five million in dividends!

In 1908 Ford produced his first Model T, the car that revolutionized automobile building because it was so simple and cheap that millions of Americans could afford it. This was the famous "Tin Lizzie," about which there were many jokes and songs. The Model T was cranked by hand, its gears were shifted by foot, its front seat had to be removed in order to fill the gasoline tank situated under the driver, and it had hard tires. The Tin Lizzie rattled and shook on the bumpy dirt roads but kept bouncing along.

Henry Ford developed a low priced automobile at Detroit and revolutionized American industrial methods with the assembly line. He sits behind the wheel of an early Ford.

Demand for these cheap cars grew so rapidly that Ford had to devise ways to manufacture them in large numbers. He developed the assembly line. Parts of a car were added to the frame as it moved along a conveyor until a completed automobile emerged at the end, ready to be driven away. This assembly-line technique was adopted by Ford's competitors and other industries. Then, in 1914 when working men's wages were very low, Ford amazed the industrial world by setting a $5.00 minimum wage for an eight-hour day. "You'll go broke," he was told repeatedly. Instead, his plant soon was working three eight-hour shifts around the clock to meet the demand for his cars.

Only an occasional Model T Ford is seen now, usually in a parade by antique car collectors, but in its time it did more to make Detroit famous than any other piece of machinery ever produced there. Today millions of sleek, powerful, and sophisticated descendants of the "flivver" and its rivals are shipped from Detroit to the rest of the world by ship, railroad, and highway.

The largest Canadian city on the Great Lakes is Toronto, the provincial capital of Ontario, situated on the north shore of Lake Ontario. With more than two million persons living in its metropolitan area, Toronto resembles the American cities on the other side of the lakes in many ways. Into its fine harbor come the raw materials of manufacturing, ore and coal, and grain from the Canadian prairies. Other materials arrive from the Canadian inland territory to the north and west. Out from the factories go an array of finished products, many of them destined for foreign countries through the St. Lawrence Seaway.

Toronto is the second largest city in Canada, surpassed only by Montreal. Unlike Montreal and Quebec, it has a relatively small French-speaking population. As with so many other Great Lakes cities, its location was dictated by the location of a river. Only in Toronto's case there are two rivers, the Don and the Humber, emptying into Lake Ontario.

The Huron Indians had a village there which they called "Toronto," meaning a place of meeting. When the British established a fort and settlement in 1794 they called it York, for the Duke of

Toronto's spectacular city hall has roused both praise and criticism. The design by Finnish architect Viljo Rewell was chosen from 532 entries.

York. Among the first settlers were British loyalists who left the new United States after the British lost the Revolutionary War. Toronto developed later than Quebec and Montreal, being incorporated in 1834. At that time the old Indian word was chosen as the new city's name. Today Toronto is a city of tall buildings and many parks, the publishing capital of Canada. Its citizens are so oriented to the thinking of their American neighbors to the south that they watch more American television programs broadcast from Buffalo, New York, sixty miles south across the lake, than Canadian broadcasts.

On the western shore of Lake Michigan stands another major city, Milwaukee, the largest in Wisconsin. When the great migration came from Europe, the Germans congregated in Milwaukee while most of the Scandinavians went on further west and north in Minnesota. At one time persons of German ancestry made up more than two-thirds of Milwaukee's population. This is no longer true. Since many Germans love beer, Milwaukee soon had many breweries and became known as the beer capital of the United

The Toronto skyline, facing Lake Ontario.

States. In the days when passenger ships sailed the Great Lakes, the trip between Milwaukee and Chicago, a hundred miles to the south, was a popular day excursion.

The metropolises that dot the Great Lakes shores have absorbed a second great migration in recent years, this one from the southern United States. Large numbers of Negroes moved north to work in Detroit's automobile plants, Cleveland's steel mills, and the factories of Chicago. Often unaccustomed to city living, they clustered together in the city ghetto areas while they adjusted to a new kind of life. Gradually they moved into other areas of the cities. Huge public housing projects are helping to provide better living quarters, and the large black populations are developing their own political and social leaders with important roles in the conduct of their cities' affairs—men like Carl Stokes of Cleveland and Richard Hatcher of Gary, who became mayors.

Nothing stands still in the Great Lakes cities. Old buildings constantly are being torn down and new ones built in their places. From the day the first immigrants arrived from Europe 150 years ago, the cities have been growing, changing, assimilating masses of persons with different backgrounds. They are beset with problems of inner city slums, unemployment, the tensions of daily life, and pollution. With all their troubles, they are nonetheless vibrant places to live, stimulating their men and women to create fresh ideas and new products for the future.

9

Lost Ships and Brave Men

Like the oceans, the fresh-water inland seas have their tales of mystery. Sailors tell of ships that vanished without a trace or succumbed to the roaring onslaughts of winds that can churn the Great Lakes into mountainous waves with hardly a moment's notice. Lake storms are worse in some respects than those on the oceans because they come on so unexpectedly. When old-time sailors began to spin yarns, one of them is almost sure to recall the disappearance of the Christmas tree ship.

Back at the turn of the twentieth century, hundreds of families in Chicago put their gifts beneath Christmas trees brought down Lake Michigan from the Upper Peninsula in a creaking, three-masted schooner, the *Rouse Simmons*. This Christmas tree ship was a tradition. About Thanksgiving each year her battered sails appeared on the horizon off the Chicago breakwater, a sure sign that the holiday season was approaching.

At the Clark Street pier in the Chicago River roustabouts unloaded the fragrant cargo of trees from the northern forests stacked high on the old wooden vessel's decks and stowed in her hold—thousands of them, each destined to brighten a home. The tight-fisted old German master of the *Rouse Simmons*, Captain

Herman Schunemann, could drive a good bargain as well as he could pilot the aging relic of the sailing ship era through the early winter storms. He sold his cargo to wholesalers who clustered around the pier.

Every year it was the same, a race to get the schooner out of the port of Manistique on the northern shore of the lake before the ice closed in for the winter, and down to Chicago with her profitable cargo. Captain Schunemann was one of the best sailors on the lake and seemed to have a sixth sense as to just how much he could make the *Rouse Simmons* do. He had sailed her so long that every noise she made as she wallowed in the seas and every flap of her canvas gave him a message.

Even the giant storm of November, 1913, did not stop the captain from making his annual voyage. Sensing an especially fat profit, he never doubted that he could nurse the vessel through any weather the lake could throw at him.

"Expect to arrive on the 27th," he wrote to a man in Chicago who handled the unloading.

At midday on the twenty-fifth of November the *Rouse Simmons* poked her bow into the rising gale outside Manistique. Captain Schunemann set her on a southerly course three hundred miles down the lake to Chicago. She was so heavily loaded with trees that the waves swept across her deck as she rolled and pitched.

During the night the storm grew worse. The captain and the first mate lashed themselves to the wheel, struggling together to hold the schooner on her course. A wave of massive proportions hit the ship broadside with such velocity that it washed part of the deck cargo into the water. Two crewmen who had been check-

TOP: Specially built for the Great Lakes, the *W.F. Fitzgerald*, a self-unloading bulk freighter built in 1906, retired several years ago.

MIDDLE: The *Christopher Columbus*, only whaleback passenger ship ever built, sailed for many years between Chicago and Milwaukee.

BOTTOM: The *Queenston* was a "canaler," a vessel unique to the Great Lakes built to go through the small canals of the pre-St. Lawrence Seaway era. She is carrying cut pulpwood, an important Canadian Great Lakes export product.

ing the lashings of the trees were swept over the rail to their deaths.

Falling temperature brought freezing. By morning the rigging, deck, and sides were covered with ice. Waves surging over the sides broke open the hatches and water drained into the hold, where it froze the trees into chunks of ice. Her sails torn, sunk low in the water by the weight of the ice, and flying distress signals, the *Rouse Simmons* was almost helpless. She kept moving south, nevertheless, pushed by the gale.

Lookout men in the tower of the United States Lifesaving Service at Sturgeon Bay, Wisconsin, spotted the ghostly white ship at noon as she drifted by offshore. They phoned ahead to another station twenty-five miles south, which sent out a surf boat in a rescue attempt. Well out in the lake, the rescuers saw the ship's icy masts jutting up through the storm. "There she is!" a man shouted. Hardly had he spoken than a swirling snow squall lashed across the water. The *Rouse Simmons* vanished into the wet white cloud. No one ever saw her again.

That Christmas many families in Chicago had to do without the delicious fragrance and heavy green boughs of northern Michigan Christmas trees. But a few weeks later the angry lake yielded a sad reminder of the *Rouse Simmons*. Commercial fishermen off the Wisconsin shore thought their nets were exceptionally heavy. When they hauled them in, they found them clogged with Christmas trees.

The Christmas tree ship was among the stubborn survivors of the age of sail on the Great Lakes. Before the wooden sailing ships, the Indians and early French explorers traveled by birchbark canoe, usually staying close to shore for safety. When the travelers did venture far out into the lakes, their flimsy craft showed excellent buoyancy. In the hands of experienced paddlers, they could survive moderately heavy weather.

The birchbark canoe was a remarkable vessel, in a primitive way. We usually think of canoes as being small craft paddled by two persons, perhaps with a third as a passenger. The canoes of the Indians and the French were far bigger and sturdier, yet light enough to be borne on the shoulders of two men on portages. Usually the canoe was about thirty-five feet long and four and a half feet wide at the center. Fully loaded, a canoe carried four tons. This was a remarkable weight when we recall that its shell was only long strips of bark, fastened together with hide thongs and pitch over a frame of saplings. Eight men usually propelled it, lustily singing rhythmic songs as they plowed ahead hour after hour. Old account books show that the men in the front and rear were paid more wages for a voyage than those in the center because they pulled more weight. For food each man received a daily allowance of one quart of mashed dried corn meal to sustain him—not much for such heavy work.

After the canoes came the sailing ships. Several of the sailboat warships that participated in Perry's victory at Put-In Bay later were converted into cargo vessels. During most of the nineteenth century the lakes were dotted with the tall masts and billowing sails of freight and passenger sailboats. In the harbors, with ships tied up close together, the masts looked like trees in a forest.

Then the steamboats came. At first these were wooden vessels much like sailing ships, carrying a full rigging of sails along with their paddle wheels amidships, driven by small engines. The first steamboat on the Great Lakes above Niagara Falls was the *Walk-in-the-Water*, so named from the description an Indian gave of seeing Robert Fulton's *Clermont* on the Hudson River. *Walk-in-the-Water* was launched at Buffalo in 1818, and soon the wood smoke from her stack became a familiar sight around Lake Erie. She had no steam whistle—it hadn't been invented yet—so her crew always fired a gun to announce her arrival and departure.

Like scores of other ships that were to come after her, the gallant little *Walk-in-the-Water* perished in a lake storm. She was caught in a gale near Buffalo in 1821 and blown onto the shore. Fortunately her crew was able to get a line ashore and tied to a tree, so all her passengers and sailors were rescued.

The steamboats grew bigger and bigger. Soon they were made of iron instead of wood and began to look something like the massive cargo vessels plying the lakes today. Their size and speed

The first steamship on the Great Lakes above Niagara Falls was the sidewheeler *Walk-in-the-Water*. Built of wood, and burning wood for fuel, the little ship survived for three years until she sank in a storm off Buffalo in 1821.

weren't enough to drive all the sailing ships out of business, nevertheless. The sailing ships had free power, the wind, and were cheap to operate. Thus a few of these old windjammers could be seen beating their way from one lake port to another with lumber and small cargoes well into the 1900's. Often they were pulled by steam vessels like barges.

The captains and owners of the passenger steamers that sailed from city to city on the Great Lakes, on regular schedules drawn almost as tightly as those of today's airliners, were proud men. They boasted of their ships' speed and were ready to gamble money on their performances. This rivalry brought about the most exciting race between ships that the Great Lakes have ever seen.

Two of the finest ships on the lakes as the new century began were the gleaming white excursion steamer *Tashmoo* of Detroit and the *City of Erie* of Cleveland. Both were side-wheelers. The idea of the race was born when the owner of the *Tashmoo* casually remarked to a newspaper reporter that he would bet $1000 his ship could beat the Cleveland ship. The Cleveland people read the story and accepted the challenge.

Preparations were made with elaborate care to assure a fair contest. The course was a 94-mile stretch of Lake Erie from Cleveland to a point off Erie, Pennsylvania. The ships were to race side by side a few miles offshore. Naturally the people who had sailed on these two ships had a special interest in them, so great cheering sections developed, much the way they do for prize-fighters before a heavyweight championship. By the day of the race, June 4, 1901, more than a million dollars had been wagered on the outcome. Thousands of Detroiters came to Cleveland to cheer the *Tashmoo*, forming part of the throng of 200,000 people who crowded the municipal pier area on the bright morning. Although an agreement by the captains of the ships forbade having passengers aboard during the race, many prominent persons with "connections" managed to get aboard as auxiliary crew members, although they hardly knew the bow from the stern.

At 9:00 a.m. the ships steamed out of the harbor, flags flying, and approached the starting line side by side. The starting gun on a tugboat was fired. Both captains ordered full throttle, causing the ships to leap forward with clouds of black coal smoke pouring from their stacks.

Since radio had not yet been invented, ingenious ways had to be found to keep the crowds on shore, and newspaper readers all over the country, posted on the progress of the race. Reporters aboard the *City of Erie* sent bulletins ashore fastened to the legs of carrier pigeons. At prearranged points they dropped messages overboard in waterproof buoys, to be picked up by motorboats and hurried ashore.

Paddle wheels churning, the ships sped eastward, pouring out smoke and steam. Five miles from the starting point their bows were cutting the water so evenly that nobody could determine the leader. The course brought them within sight of shore at Fairport

This old photograph depicts an exciting event which took place on Lake Erie in June of 1901. Beneath a cloud of black smoke, the *City*

Harbor, twenty-five miles east of Cleveland, so the little city's schools were closed for the day to let the students see the excitement. A crowd of fifty thousand gathered there.

Still, the *Tashmoo* and the *City of Erie* were so close that many on shore could see no difference. Their paddlewheels were revolving more than thirty times a minute, creating a boiling wake. But a motor launch reached shore with a bulletin, "*City of Erie* falling behind!" The *Tashmoo* built up a lead of two lengths, about six hundred feet. This was short-lived. As the ships reached deeper water, a slight design defect in the *Tashmoo* became apparent at top speed. She "squatted" down at the stern. This increased her drag in the water. Frantically the crew dragged everything loose on deck up to the bow, even two grand pianos from the lounge, in an attempt to get her level in the water. In vain—at Conneaut, Ohio, the *City of Erie* had moved in front by a length.

Then luck turned against the leader. The helmsman of the *City of Erie* fainted from excitement and the big wheel spun from his hands. Momentarily the ship wobbled until another man could leap to the post. Once more the noses of the ships were virtually

of Erie, at the far right, crosses the finish line ahead of the *Tashmoo*, far left, in the Great Lakes' most famous race.

even, after more than three hours. Down below in the engine room, the *City of Erie* had another crisis. A spring broke on a valve, so that steam escaped and reduced the engine's power. The chief engineer concocted a unique emergency repair job. He ordered a tiny 125-pound crew member, Johnny Eaton, to sit on top of the hot valve lid, protected only by a cushion of waste rags, and hold it in place with his body. Tortured by the heat, he clung to his perch as the pistons churned on. Other crewmen doused him with buckets of water to relieve the pain. Perspiring and writhing, he was still on the hot seat as the ships reached the finish.

Off Erie, the steamer *America* served as the official finish line. Those aboard her thought the racers were nose to nose as they approached on the western horizon in a cloud of smoke. But the *City of Erie* was showing her superiority. She swept past the finish line forty-five seconds ahead of the *Tashmoo* amid the welcoming whistles and bells of small craft. After four hours and twenty minutes of racing along a course of ninety-four miles the victor won by three lengths, less than a thousand feet! Down in the engine room, Johnny Eaton staggered to a bin of crushed ice that had been used to cool the condenser. He sat down in it with a grin of relief.

Trips on Great Lakes steamers were a popular form of travel for many decades. In addition to the regularly scheduled service between cities, daily and weekend excursion trips provided vacation outings during the Gay Nineties and for many years after. There were longer cruises, too, lasting a week or more, but most "trippers" piled aboard ships like the *Tashmoo* that were built especially for the one-day excursion trade, with few overnight cabins. Bunting flying, whistles tooting, these ships carried thousands on outings to scenic points around the lakes, then home again at night. There were moonlight cruises as well—short evening trips in summer with dancing on deck and romantic couples leaning against the railing, watching the moonbeams on the waves.

One of these happy day excursions, on the steamer *Eastland*, resulted in the worst tragedy ever to happen on the Great Lakes, in which 835 persons drowned. Almost unbelievably, the disaster happened before the ship had even left her berth in the Chicago River.

The year was 1915. The *Eastland* was a well-patronized excursion ship, tall and white and 269 feet long. The previous year she had carried more than 200,000 persons on trips around the lakes. Near the stern she had a steam calliope that entertained the passengers with shrill tunes like a circus show. On the morning of July 24, she was taking aboard hundreds of families from a Chicago industrial firm bound for a picnic on the dunes at Michigan City, Indiana, sixty miles away.

About 2500 men, women, and children had crowded aboard. The band played welcoming songs. The holiday makers carried picnic baskets, baseballs and bats, and other equipment for a day of fun.

"Look, we're leaving," somebody called as the gangplank was hauled in. A tugboat churned into position to pull the vessel out into the river. Hundreds of passengers moved to the left side to watch the action. Slowly at first, then more rapidly, the deck began tilting. Nobody was alarmed for a minute or two. As the tilt

When the excursion steamer *Eastland* capsized in the Chicago River,
835 persons drowned. Hundreds of others were saved in rescue opera-
tions shown here.

became extreme, fright seized the crowd. They tried scrambling
back to the shore side, but the pitch was too steep. With a sucking
sound the *Eastland* toppled over on her side in twenty-one feet of
water, her starboard side rising fifteen feet above the surface.

Hundreds were thrown into the water. Some lucky ones
grabbed furniture and boxes to stay afloat. Others were dragged
to their death under the surface. Those who had gone into the
cabins and lounges were trapped and drowned before they knew
what was happening. People on shore a few yards away gasped in
horror.

Long official investigations and court action followed, to determine the cause. The blame finally was placed on a ship's engineer
whose duty it was to keep the ship's water ballast tanks, which
held eight hundred tons, properly trimmed to maintain stability.

He failed to do his job that midsummer morning and more than eight hundred people perished because of his negligence.

Trapped in the silt at the bottom of the lakes is the wreckage of many ships that didn't make it to port. How much wealth is concealed in those wrecks nobody can guess. There is known to be approximately $97,000 in cash in one of them, waiting for lucky and ingenious divers to capture.

In 1841 an immigrant steamboat, the *Erie*, carrying Norwegian and German settlers to new homes in the Midwest, sank in Lake Erie off Silver Creek, New York. The *Erie* was known to carry $100,000, mostly money the three hundred immigrants had brought along to buy homesteads. Thirteen years after the *Erie* went to the bottom in forty-eight feet of water, divers tried to salvage the lost wealth. They found the ship and recovered $2,000 in coins. More than a hundred years passed, until in 1960 scuba divers located the wreckage again and brought up about a thousand dollars in foreign currency. The bulk of the money escaped them, however, and still lies in the wreckage.

A scuba diver in 1967 found the remains of a ship on the bottom of Green Bay, not far from where Jean Nicolet landed. It rested in 110 feet of water, a mysterious relic of the past. Volunteers working weekends and on vacations for two years brought up old coins and other souvenirs. They pumped silt out of the sunken hull and succeeded in running cables under it through the mud. A salvage barge was stationed above the wreck, the cables were attached to it, and the boat was hoisted close to the surface. Still slung under the salvage vessel, it was towed to the harbor of Manistee and hauled to the surface by crane.

But what ship was it? Old records showed that a ship named the *Alvin Clark* sank in that part of the Green Bay at the height of the Civil War in 1864. The recovered ship was a 110-foot long, two-masted schooner that fitted the *Alvin Clark*'s description. With her 60-foot masts replaced, she needed little more than a new canvas to sail the lakes again.

Today the big passenger ships have disappeared from the Great Lakes. Except for the ferry boats that carry freight cars and automobiles across Lake Michigan, and a few other short-distance ferry convenience services, passenger trade is a thing of the past. Nobody wanted to ride the inter-city ships and the excursion steamers any longer; people could reach their destinations faster and more easily in their own automobiles, or by flying. So a colorful era has ended.

One of the last passenger ships to sail the Great Lakes, the S.S. *Keewatin*, is preserved as a marine museum at Saugatuck, Michigan, so people of later generations can see what life on these ships was like. The *Keewatin* sailed from Georgian Bay at the eastern corner of Lake Huron to Fort William at the western end of Lake Superior for the Canadian Pacific Railroad for fifty-seven years, until 1965. Instead of being scrapped as most outdated ships were, she was towed to Saugatuck. With accommodations for 288 passengers, the 336-foot-long *Keewatin* had hand-carved oak panels, a long flower-filled lounge, a ballroom, and other touches of luxury. Visitors today see her staterooms made up and her dining-room tables set with linen and silver, ready to sail on a trip she probably will never make again.

All that's left on the Great Lakes are the cargo ships, and what giant ships they are! They are more massive, faster, and busier than ever.

The *Keewatin* was one of the last passenger ships to sail the Great Lakes. After fifty-seven years of service she was converted into a marine museum at Saugatuck, Michigan. This picture shows the *Keewatin* in the 1930's.

Specially designed ships carry enormous amounts of raw materials. Iron ore dug from the open pit mines of the Upper Peninsula and Minnesota is transported to the steel mills at the lower end of Lake Michigan, or to Cleveland and other Lake Erie ports. From there some of it is hauled overland to Pittsburgh. The Great Northern ore docks at Superior, Wisconsin, are the largest in the world. Ore from the pits of the Mesabi Range is carried to the docks in long freight trains. A train pulls onto the elevated tracks of the docks. The bottoms of its hopper cars are opened and the ore tumbles with a roar down into the storage space. From there it is loaded into the ships' holds through chutes. An ore boat of the size generally in use during the early 1970's could swallow up the contents of a 180-car train, more than thirteen thousand tons, in a thirty-minute loading period.

From early spring until the ice closes in, the ore boats travel back and forth. Many carry their own unloading equipment, a large crane-like apparatus built above the holds. A ship sails up to a dock, turns its self-unloading equipment into position, and soon a stream of cargo stored in the spacious holds—iron ore, golden grain from the Canadian wheatfields, or limestone from the quar-

Taconite agglomorates pour into the holds of the *B.F. Affleck*, through multiple chutes at Duluth, for movement to the company's steel mills. Early spring ice still jams the harbor.

Wheat from the Canadian prairies is stored at Thunder Bay, Ontario, at the western end of Lake Superior, then loaded aboard ships for movement to many ports of the world.

ries of northeastern Michigan—is pouring onto the docks or into storage bins.

Although most of the iron ore is for use in the United States, much of the grain is destined for other countries, to be turned into bread for people in many parts of the world. A typical Great Lakes grain boat carries nearly a half-million bushels of wheat, so much that thirty freight trains of sixty-five cars each would be needed to haul it overland. Approximately 4,500,000 loaves of bread can be made from the cargo of just one ship! Long lines of grain elevators rise like windowless skyscrapers above such harbors as Thunder Bay, Ontario, the world's largest grain storage center, for loading; Chicago, for transshipment; Buffalo, New York, for loading onto barges on the New York Barge Canal; Toronto and Montreal, either for processing into flour or for shipment onto the oceans.

In the early days Great Lakes cargo ships were designed somewhat like passenger ships with the engines, captain's bridge, and superstructure amidships. A few years after the Civil War two thousand sailing vessels were carrying cargo around the lakes. Then a basic change was made in design. The bridge and cabins were built at the front, the engine room at the stern. The long space in between was all cargo holds. The longer the ships grew, the bigger the line of holds. For awhile freight ships called "whalebacks" were a frequent sight on the lakes. These vessels had blunt noses and looked like long metal cigars low in the water.

Early in the 1970's an ore carrier was built at Erie, Pennsylvania, that dwarfed other ships on the lakes. The bow and stern sections were constructed at Pascagoula, Mississippi, and welded together. This strange foreshortened vessel sailed 2600 miles up the Atlantic Ocean, up the St. Lawrence River, through Lake Ontario and the Welland Canal to Erie.

A vertical line had been painted on its sides, between bow and

Largest ship on the Great Lakes is the ore carrier *Stewart J. Cort*. The bow and stern were built in Mississippi, welded together, and sailed to Erie, Pennsylvania. BELOW: At Erie, shipbuilders "cut along the dotted line" and inserted the prefabricated hold sections, so that the ship looked like this as she passed the Detroit skyline on her maiden voyage.

stern, and a joker had written, "Cut Along the Dotted Line." The shipbuilders at Erie did just that—they cut the stubby ship apart and inserted prefabricated sections of hold between them like books between bookends. When all the sections were welded together, there was a 67,610-ton ship a thousand feet long, the *Stewart J. Cort*. This ship can carry 57,000 tons of pelletized iron each trip from Lake Superior to the mills on Lake Michigan and Lake Erie—twice as much as any previous lake ship—and unload the entire cargo with its own endless belt in less than five hours.

Even such mammoth ships face the perils of Great Lakes weather. When a sudden November storm sweeps out of the northeast across Lake Huron with swirling snow and waves thirty feet high, the captains and crews must show bravery and skill lest their vessels smash to bits and join the hundreds of others that have sunk to their doom since La Salle's *Griffin* went to the bottom three hundred years ago.

10

War Beneath the Waves

While pleasure sailboats and cargo ships cut through the waves on the Great Lakes' surface, a fascinating and deadly war is being fought in the depths below. Fish by the billions struggle for survival in the cold dark waters, not merely against the sport and commercial fishermen who try to hook or net them but against each other.

This underwater world turns black beneath the depth of two hundred feet. In the area between the surface sunlight and the blackness, gloomy twilight gradually turns into night as the depth increases. Here in the eerie silence a twenty-pound salmon twitches its tail, lunges forward and swallows an alewife weighing a few ounces. An eel-like sea lamprey fastens its suction-cup mouth onto the flank of a lake trout, chewing a fatal hole in its side. The primeval battle goes on endlessly. Up above, men catch only glimpses of the struggle. Yet their own actions, both heedless ones and those that have been planned scientifically, have influenced it enormously.

When the great ice cap withdrew from the region, the newly formed Great Lakes became much like the bottom of a saucer. The water draining into them from several directions brought

ABOVE: This picture shows the circular mouth of the sea lamprey with its short, sharp teeth, and the damage it has inflicted on a fish.

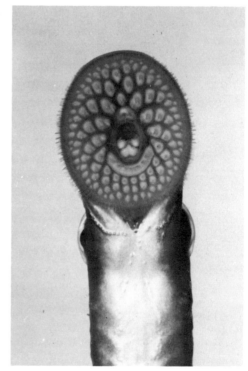

Close-up of the suction-cup mouth of a sea lamprey

many kinds of fish to establish their homes in the cold fresh water. Some species made their way into the lakes down streams from the Arctic; others came from rivers draining the midwestern prairies.

More than 230 species of fish found a home in the lakes. Aquatic plants developed in the water, and insects like the mayflies became thick. Insect eggs, plant life, and millions of tiny plant particles and microscopic animals in the water provided food for most of the fish. Along the lake bottoms the sturgeon, whose eggs someday would become caviar on the tables of the Russian czars, ate snails and clams. Sturgeon do not breed until they are about twenty years old and they live about a hundred years. The muskellunge weighing sixty pounds—the giant "muskies" of fishermen's lore—prowled through the shallow thickets of aquatic plants. These huge fish ate other fish, and frogs, mice, and ducklings as well. At various levels in the lakes the waters abounded in whitefish, ciscoes, yellow walleye, blue pike, and scores of other species.

Among them were predators such as the lake trout and burbot, that obtained their food by eating other fish. Untouched and uninfluenced by man, a natural food chain developed in the lakes. Some fish found sustenance from plants, others from tiny animal and insect life. The predator fish in turn devoured these fish.

The Great Lakes became potentially a fisherman's delight, but for thousands of years there were no fishermen there to enjoy the sport. The few Indians who came to live around the lakes caught all the fish they needed with relatively little trouble during the warm months. In the tumbling waters of the St. Marys River between Lakes Superior and Huron they clubbed and caught so many whitefish that they soon had more than they could eat at a feast. Even so, this made no dent at all in the fish population or nature's food chain.

Among the seldom-found fish in the Great Lakes are some considered to be "living fossils"; that is, species unknown or virtually unknown on other continents, such as the paddlefish and mooneye. The great depths of Lake Superior, a quarter mile in some places, represent waters that are "new," with conditions almost like those in existence when the last glacier withdrew.

The first white men to visit the lakes were astounded at the number of fish and the ease of catching them. Many kinds of lake fish swim up the tributary rivers or gather in the shallows near shore to spawn. The pioneers found these spawning grounds and attacked the swarms of fish with many kinds of weapons—pitchforks, axes, clubs, spears, nets, and guns. At the American fort built on the Maumee River in Ohio, upstream from Lake Erie, soldiers in the garrison frequently caught a thousand fish in an afternoon. And the fish stories grew. My, how they grew! There was a claim that in some ponds the fish were so thick that a blind man could throw a spear into the water and hit a fish nine times out of ten.

But, as so often happens, the white men were greedy.

Commercial fishing developed as cities grew around the lakes. For a long time there was no control over what kinds of fish were caught, and when and how many. Hundreds of tons of choice fish were hauled up in nets year after year, faster than the fish could breed to replace themselves. No artificial "planting" of infant fish was done to restock the waters. Eventually the Great Lakes were overfished, so that supplies of such desirable food as whitefish and lake trout dwindled. The natural underwater food chain was upset. Conditions were ripe for a disaster.

It came, in the form of an unpleasant-looking creature called the sea lamprey.

A commercial fisherman working in the eastern waters of Lake Erie late in 1921 hauled in a whitefish and found attached to its side another fish that resembled a piece of gray garden hose about a foot and a half long. When he pulled the creature's mouth free from the whitefish, he found that it was filled with a circular set of sharp, short teeth. This was the first recorded discovery of the sea lamprey in the lakes above Niagara Falls. What followed in the next quarter century was nearly the death of Great Lakes commercial and large-scale sport fishing.

Although it looks like an eel, the sea lamprey isn't one because

A sea lamprey has attached itself to the side of a chinook salmon, sinking its circular set of teeth into the large fish with a death grip.

of a different mouth structure, lacking upper and lower jaws. Originally it was a salt-water inhabitant but worked its way up the St. Lawrence River into Lake Ontario. There it adapted itself to live in fresh water. After the Welland Canal was opened, establishing a stair-step water route from Lake Ontario to Lake Erie, sea lampreys worked their way through its locks into Erie. Some years later they reached Lake Huron. In the deep cold water of Huron the lampreys flourished. The abundance of lake trout, whitefish, burbot, and ciscoes gave them an easy food supply. Multiplying at an astonishing rate, lampreys committed mass murder underwater. At times fishermen hauled up dead lake trout to which four or five lamprey had attached themselves.

Soon the lampreys had slithered through the Straits of Mackinac into Lake Michigan, and then into Lake Superior in limited numbers. The barrier formed by the locks at Sault Ste. Marie slowed their migration into the far lake. At the height of commercial fishing in Lakes Huron and Michigan, the annual catch of lake trout was an enormous eleven million pounds a year. By 1950 it had fallen to 500,000 pounds because of the way the lampreys had diminished the trout population.

ABOVE: Sea lampreys as well as ships make their way up the St. Lawrence Seaway. Here, two ships are at Lock #4 of the Welland Canal, one upbound, one downbound.

A sea lamprey nest at spawning time

Each spring the lamprey swim up the streams emptying into the Great Lakes to spawn and die. A single female can deposit more than sixty thousand eggs. These eggs sink into the muddy stream beds, where they remain at least four years before developing into adults and going down into the lakes. After this, the adult lamprey has only a year of life before going upstream for spawning.

Nature's balance was thrown entirely out of kilter by the lamprey. By killing the lake trout and burbot they removed most of the traditional predator fish from the lakes. They themselves ignore small fish, the kinds the predators devour. Thus a great gap in the food chain was created.

Into this gap by the billions swam an obnoxious little fish with a strange name, the alewife. People around the lakes, especially Lake Michigan, soon came to know the alewife all too well. Just why it happened isn't clear, but alewives died off in masses near the shore in spring and summer of some years. The stench they created was horrible.

Like the sea lamprey, the alewife originally was an Atlantic Ocean species. It entered fresh-water streams to spawn. It, too, reached Lake Ontario, worked its way through the Welland Canal locks, and entered Lake Erie. Needing deep water in winter, the alewives found Lakes Huron, Michigan, and Superior more to their liking than shallow Lake Erie. Since relatively few predators were left in these lakes to devour them, they multiplied at an amazing speed. The first alewife was caught in Lake Michigan in 1949. Seventeen years later, when conservation men made test trawls in the lake, the catch they hauled up was 80 per cent alewives!

If men were ever to restore nature's underwater balance, it was obvious that first they must control the sea lamprey. He was the villian, the alewife the nuisance.

The logical place to attack the lampreys was in the tributary rivers where they came to spawn. Weirs were built to trap them in the rivers, with only moderate success. So fishery experts enlisted the help of chemists. They asked, "Can you develop a compound

137

LEFT: A catch of over three tons of alewives was taken in a fifteen-minute trawl drag from Chicago harbor by the research vessel *KAHO* in May, 1966.

BELOW: A mechanical weir in a tributary of Lake Huron

RIGHT: Downstream trap to catch sea lampreys, in a tributary of Lake Superior.

BELOW RIGHT: Biologist measuring a sea lamprey.

that will kill lampreys without harming other fish?" The request was a hard one. For six years the chemists tested different combinations, nearly six thousand in all, until they developed a chemical that did exactly what the conservationists requested. The method was

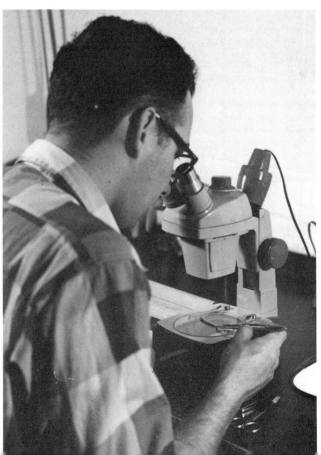

to poison the adult lampreys before they had time to spawn, so that over a few years the population would decline.

That is how it worked out. By the early 1960's the count of lampreys at the river weirs was falling dramatically. There still are lampreys in the Great Lakes but their number can be kept under satisfactory control by continued effort.

The alewife problem remained and kept getting worse. An alewife is a "junk" fish, good only for grinding up into pet food and fish meal. An individual dead alewife is inconspicuous, six inches long and weighing two or three ounces. But when gathered in masses, as they usually are, alewives are a formidable, stinking mess.

This fish lives on tiny food organisms in the water, which it sucks in through a filter so efficient that it has an important advantage over other small fish in the eternal battle for food.

Alewives don't like cold water. When winter comes and the surface freezes, they swim down into the depths where the water is warmer. If the temperature of the water falls below 38 degrees Fahrenheit they die, a fact that has restricted their development in Lake Superior.

In the spring the alewives rise toward the surface in gigantic schools, bullying their way through the home waters of other small fish by sheer weight of numbers. As the summer nears, the alewives move closer to shore and to the surface. Then the phenomenon of mass death occurs. This does not appear to be connected with spawning; in fact, many alewives die before they spawn.

The die-offs vary in intensity from year to year, but nobody is sure why this happens. Scientists who have studied the strange habits of the alewives speculate that the difference between their original ocean environment and their existence in the fresh-water lakes may be responsible in some way for the deaths. Despite their abundance, according to this theory, the alewives haven't fully adapted to lake life and are affected by the temperature changes. Examination of alewives taken from the ocean and those taken from the lakes shows that the thyroid glands are much less devel-

During the mass die-offs of alewives in the 1960's, millions of the little fish washed ashore, clogging beaches and creating a ferocious stench.

oped in the lake specimens. Perhaps this is because salt water has a much higher content of iodine than fresh water. It may be that inadequate thyroid in certain combinations of season and temperature influence the massive deaths. Whatever the cause, the result is miserable.

The worst die-off of all happened in southern Lake Michigan in the summer of 1967. Billions of alewives floated onto the shore and into harbor waters, creating such an odor and mess that many beaches had to be closed to swimmers and boaters. Bulldozers scooped up mounds of fish, then buried them. Boats dredged them from the water but the weight often broke the nets. In one fifteen-minute period, more than three tons of alewives were pulled from the Chicago harbor by a single dragnet. Masses of fish clogged the intakes of water systems in lake cities. In some harbor entrances they were so thick at times that it seemed a man could walk across the channel on top of them. The slimy, silvery horde drove men from parts of the lake shore, just as it had taken control of the waters where desirable fish once flourished.

At the very time when the alewife menace was at its worst, however, rescue was on its way. The underwater war entered a new phase, this time brought about by man intentionally.

Having upset the lakes' ancient balance by overfishing, men set about trying to recreate the natural food chain. With the lampreys under control, the task was to get predator fish back into the waters so they could eat the alewives. Conservationists had wisely collected lake-trout eggs from Lake Superior in the late 1940's and developed stocks of the trout in fisheries. During the 1960's several million young fish a year were released and, with their lamprey enemies largely eradicated, they multiplied. The whitefish began to increase again, too.

"But that isn't enough," fishery experts said. "Too much damage has been done. Let's try to stock the lakes with sturdy big fish that have never lived in them before."

They went to the Pacific Ocean for infant coho and chinook salmon, both of which spawn in freshwater streams along the coast but spend most of their lives in open ocean. With such habits, could the salmon adapt themselves to an entirely freshwater life? Nearly a million young salmon, five to seven inches long, were released into Lake Superior and upper Lake Michigan in the spring of 1966 as an experiment.

Not only did these salmon survive in their new habitat, they flourished. Just a hundred days after the little ones were planted, a fisherman hauled in a coho salmon on his line. It had grown two and a half times in length and ten times in weight during that short interval. Less than two years after the first planting, fishermen were catching coho weighing as much as twenty-five pounds.

The predatory salmon, it turned out, love to eat alewives. They sweep through a school of the "junk" fish, snapping their jaws shut on their victims with delight. Fishermen report hauling in large coho with the remains of four or five alewives in their stomachs. The slower growing, larger chinook salmon, which weigh about fifty pounds when mature, behave in the same way. As a bonus,

Happy fisherman displays a coho salmon caught in Lake Michigan. These salmon were planted in the lake as infants and feed on masses of alewives in the waters.

the coho will even eat adult lampreys.

Once again a natural food chain was developing in the lakes, and with it came a bonanza for sport fishermen. Salmon fishing has become a lively new Great Lakes sport, especially in Lake Michigan. Sometimes fishermen take coho on lines cast from piers near downtown Chicago; at other seasons the fish are found in abundance ten miles out in the lake. At spawning time the salmon swim up the tributary rivers and with remarkable strength hurl themselves across dams, just as their brothers in the oceans do.

The alewife population in the lakes has diminished remarkably. No great die-offs like that of 1967 have occurred since the salmon began to mature, although dead fish by the hundreds still float along the shore every summer. Now some experts are wondering —will the growing throngs of salmon destroy so many alewives that the big fish in turn run short of food? Probably not soon, if at all, most fisheries men believe. Meanwhile, other species of fish

Chinook salmon weighing as much as fifty pounds have been caught in Lake Michigan. Like the coho salmon, they were planted there as infants, and feed on schools of alewives in the lake.

When the coho are running in Lake Michigan, thousands of fishermen turn out for the sport, bringing in large catches.

that had been decreased by lamprey attacks or squeezed out by the alewives are making a comeback. Once more the Great Lakes are winning renown for their fishing, returning to conditions that existed thirty or forty years ago. Having almost destroyed the desirable fish life of the lakes by his greed, man has saved it by his scientific ingenuity.

II

The Patient Assassin

On a summer afternoon the waters of Lake Erie are bright and busy—cargo vessels move into the harbors, power boats zip along the shore; farther out, fishing craft haul in their catches. This is the lake some experts on ecology call "dead." Yet it seems very much alive. So what are they talking about?

Look more closely, and the explanation emerges. Swimming is forbidden at some beaches because the polluted water is dangerous to health. An 800-mile-square patch of algae grows in the western end of the lake. Scummy industrial wastes flow into the lake from the tributary rivers; inadequately treated sewage fouls the water. Even these fairly evident signs of how men abuse the lake don't tell all of the story. Former Secretary of the Interior Stewart Udall called pollution in Lake Erie a "patient assassin which chokes its victims ever so slowly and silently."

Lake Erie is the most notorious case of water pollution in North America, reflected in lesser degree in the other Great Lakes and all bodies of water threatened by man's heedlessness and greed. Because, despite the first impression that everything is normal, Lake Erie is a sick, sick lake. Those who call it dead exaggerate. It can still be saved, but long, strenuous efforts are necessary. Even

The polluted condition of the Cuyahoga River is shown in this photograph, taken on Whiskey Island.

bottom and spreading in a choking green mass offshore. In normal amounts, algae have a role in the chain of nature. Trouble arises when the growth of algae is overstimulated by excessive amounts of phosphates dumped into the water. Under undisturbed conditions, nature puts a sufficient amount of phosphorus material into the water to permit the existence of some algae. Exposed to a continuing overrich diet of phosphates, algae run wild with disastrous results. They choke water intake pipes and clog the propellors of boats. When algae die they sink to the bottom as debris, giving off a rotten-egg smell of hydrogen sulfide.

Worse yet, the mass of algae consume oxygen from the water, throwing nature's processes out of balance. The highly desirable sturgeon and whitefish that once thrived in Lake Erie cannot survive without sufficient oxygen. Fish that seek the colder waters at the bottom of the lake have suffered especially because the lack of oxygen is severe in the lower water levels where the mass of dead algae and other man-induced matter accumulates.

Nevertheless fishing boats still take large hauls from the lake, a fact that seems inconsistent. The explanation is that carp and other coarse fish that can tolerate pollution have replaced the more sensitive fish that were prized for their taste and sportiness. Most fish caught commercially in Lake Erie today are sold for cat and dog food.

Household detergents reach the lake mostly through the discharge from sewer plants of the cities ringing the shore, carried there in the runoff water from each home. Since 13 million people live around the lake, 11.5 million on the American side and 1.5 million on the Canadian side, this detergent concentration is huge. The phosphorus content of Lake Erie more than tripled in the twenty years after phosphate detergents were introduced in the 1940's. A study by a joint Canada-United States commission found that Lake Ontario is suffering from the speeded-up aging process in the same way that Lake Erie is, but less intensely. It found that in the test year, 1967, 52.9 million pounds of phosphorus were dumped into the two lakes. A large part of this entered through municipal sewage. On the American side of the lakes, 70 per cent of the phosphorus in the sewage originated from detergents and on the Canadian side, 50 per cent.

This heavy influx of phosphorus products can be reduced in two ways. More complicated sewage treatment plants can be built that are able to remove approximately 90 per cent of the phosphates from the runoff water. Or rules can be adopted forbidding the use of detergents containing phosphates. Both methods are being attempted. Bigger, more efficient sewage treatment plants are being built. Over the opposition of the detergent manufacturers, laws have been proposed—and in some cases passed—that forbid the sale of detergents containing phosphates after certain dates, or limiting the percentage of phosphates permitted in a detergent product.

Even if the flow of phosphates into Lake Erie through sewage systems could be stopped completely, phosphorus would still reach the water although in much reduced quantities. Land that was forest or meadow when the Europeans came to the lake is now farmland, rich and productive. The more excavation and cultivation, and the more erosion, there is in this farmland, the greater the amount of silt that washes into the lake. When rural areas are broken up for suburban housing, more silt is turned loose. At Toledo, Ohio, the Maumee River dumps three tons of silt a minute into the lake. Not only does this silt slowly fill the bottom of the lake and make the water murky, but it carries heavy amounts of phosphates and nitrogen from farm fertilizers and other agricultural sources.

"Stop the use of chemical fertilizers," the conservationists say.

"But that will reduce crops when we need more of them to feed our growing population," the farmers retort. "And it would raise the price of food."

There is still another danger from the chemicals, oil, and silt that pour into the lake. These discharges have raised the temperature of Erie's waters two degrees since 1920, threatening the survival of such temperature-sensitive fish as yellow perch.

Lake Erie is the most polluted of the Great Lakes because it is the shallowest of the five, holding the least water, with the largest surrounding population in relation to its size. Its western end, where the maximum depth of the water is only sixty feet, has the worst pollution. The eastern end, which is more than three times as deep, has the least.

Nine-tenths of Lake Erie's water reaches it through the Detroit River at the northwest corner, coming down as through a funnel from Lake Huron through the St. Clair River, Lake St. Clair, and the Detroit River. When the water flows down from Lake Huron into this funnel it is clear and relatively pure. By the time it spreads out into Lake Erie, seventy-seven miles to the south, it has accumulated the discharges of a great industrial area. For many years it carried an appalling amount of filth. The chemical plants at Sarnia, Ontario, poured their industrial wastes into the river. At

Detroit, sewage from the city flowed into the stream. The river that carries the parade of ships down into Lake Erie also carried dissolved and undissolved sewage laden with phosphates and other chemicals, organic matter, and oil. These impurities dropped into the western basin of Lake Erie.

By the middle 1960's scientists and conservation spokesmen were alerting the public. Pressure developed, far later than it should have done, to reduce the damaging flow of filth. The cities and industries undertook to build a billion dollars' worth of adequate treatment plants. The United States government applied its power especially against the cities of Detroit and Cleveland, which were the worst offenders. Once, in 1971, the inadequate sewage plant at Cleveland failed to function temporarily, dumping five million gallons of raw sewage an hour into the lake. Beaches had to be closed for nearly a hundred miles east of the city.

When satisfactory sewage plants have been completed, years will be required before the lake can cleanse itself partially by the flow-through of water from the western to the eastern end, and over Niagara Falls. Today, a heavy burden of pollution passes over the falls and into Lake Ontario. Even with sewage dumping controlled and phosphates reduced, other man-made threats to Lake Erie's water quality will remain.

One of these is mercury. This silvery substance, the only metal to occur in liquid form at natural earth temperatures, appears at many points in our environment without assistance from man, in the water or the oceans and in the soil. It is released into the atmosphere when coal is burned. And it is found in fish. The United States Food and Drug Administration rules that the safe amount of mercury in a fish that is to be eaten by a human is .5 part per million. When excessive amounts of mercury are consumed by a person, damage to his nervous system can result, sometimes bringing on insanity. In the nineteenth century, for example, when men wore felt hats, mercury compounds used to treat the felt were absorbed by hat workers, who became mentally ill. This led to the phrase "mad as a hatter"—hence the "Mad

Mercury pollution became a danger in portions of the Great Lakes, leading to this official warning.

FISH FOR FUN

FISHERMEN...

FOR THE PROTECTION
OF YOUR HEALTH...
FISH FROM THESE WATERS
SHOULD NOT BE EATEN
BECAUSE OF MERCURY
CONTAMINATION.

ONTARIO DEPARTMENT OF LANDS AND FORESTS
HON. RENE BRUNELLE   G. H. U. BAYLY
MINISTER   DEPUTY MINISTER

Hatter" in Lewis Carroll's *Alice's Adventures in Wonderland.*

At several points around the Great Lakes, industries using mercury in their manufacturing processes dumped it into the river tributaries, or directly into the lakes. This was particularly true along the waterway from Lake Huron to Lake Erie. Since mercury is thirteen and a half times as heavy as water, the companies assumed that it would sink to the bottom of the lakes and remain there, causing no danger.

In the spring of 1970 a graduate student at Western Ontario University who was studying the effects of mercury tested fish in Lake St. Clair. He found levels of mercury in some of them as high as 7.09 parts per million, fourteen times the stated safety limit. Word of his discovery caused an official uproar. Both the Province of Ontario and the State of Michigan shut down Lake St. Clair to commercial fishing and Ohio did the same to part of Lake Erie. Sport fishermen were warned not to eat the fish they caught because of the poison danger.

The dumpers, in assuming that mercury on the bottom of the lakes was safe, had overlooked a chemical reaction called organic complexing. They were abusing the chain of life without realizing it. Especially when water is polluted with human and industrial sewage, as Lake St. Clair and Lake Erie were, mercury in the water is turned into an organic salt, toxic methyl mercury, by bacteria. Algae consume the bacteria. Small plankton in the water feed on the algae, larger plankton on the smaller ones, small fish on the large plankton, larger fish on the smaller ones. Finally, men catch and eat the fish. The mercury climbs right up the ladder of aquatic life into men's stomachs.

At this point another discovery was made that showed how long the mercury content in the lake waters had been building up. The New York State Museum had kept a number of fish in preserved form for display, some of them more than forty years old. A check of fish caught in 1927 showed that they contained one part per million of mercury, double the official safety limit. Yet they had not been exposed at close range to the kind of industrial mercury dumping that was blamed for the Lake St. Clair scare. Made aware of the danger, industrial plants found other ways to dispose of their mercury waste than dumping it in water. Within a year, nearly 90 per cent of such dumping had ceased. Unfortunately, while this prevented a worsening of the danger, it did not remove the peril automatically because of the long life of methyl mercury. Mercury dumping into the Buffalo River at the eastern end of Lake Erie ceased in 1960, but tests ten years later showed that samples of plankton, algae, and sediment taken from the mouth of the river contained as much mercury as similar samples at the earlier date. A long time will pass before the mercury danger to fish in Lake Erie disappears, despite the belated halt in dumping. There is no known quick way to eliminate the contamination that exists; perhaps nature will find a way, but so far men haven't. Reduction in the amount of algae through a cleanup of sewage contamination should help.

While Erie is the most polluted of the Great Lakes, ecologists also are concerned about the southern part of Lake Michigan, where heavy population and industry are concentrated in an

Water pollution can kill even large fish, as shown by this picture taken in Wisconsin.

urban band from Milwaukee around the curve of the shore past Chicago to Gary, Indiana. Lake Michigan does not have the natural flow-through of water that Lakes Huron, Erie, and Ontario do. Chicago's sewage is discharged into the Chicago River, whose flow has been reversed into the Mississippi River drainage system rather than into Lake Michigan. This helps the situation, but inadequately treated sewage is discharged into the lake from Wisconsin cities. Heavy amounts of industrial waste are dumped into tributary streams and into the lake itself in the Chicago-Gary area. Beaches at points around the southern end of Lake Michigan have been closed to swimmers from time to time because of pollution. Lead, arsenic, cyanide, and zinc are among the chemicals found in tests of the water and sediment near Chicago. Under pressure from federal and state governments, a slow cleanup of these pollutants has begun.

The insidious pall of pollution has even discolored the water of

Green Bay where Jean Nicolet stepped ashore from his canoe, thinking it was China. In that day, and for three hundred years afterward, Green Bay was clean. However, along the Fox River, which enters the bay at its head, through the city of Green Bay, is the greatest concentration of paper and pulp mills in the world. The discharges from these mills and other industries have been sending a plume of pollution farther into the bay each year. The same telltale signs found in Lake Erie—lack of oxygen in the water and the growth of algae—appeared in Green Bay.

Cleanest and purest of the Great Lakes is Lake Superior. There is less population and industry around its shore, and its volume of water is so immense that the pollutants entering it are dispersed.

Superior has had a pollution problem of a different kind than those experienced in other lakes. A plant built to extract iron pellets from taconite ore dug on the Mesabi Range at the western end of the lake dumped 67,000 tons of waste from the processed ore into the lake every day, an enormous amount in a year's time. Critics of the practice pointed out that it muddied the water and led to the growth of algae. This had gone on for about fifteen years before the federal government gave the company notice to find a better way to dispose of its waste matter.

Since the public became aware of the damage being done to the lakes by pollution, and environmental experts showed that unless something was done two or more of the lakes might degenerate into oversize sewers, publicity and the anger of citizens have been reaping results. The day of reckless, who-cares pollution of the lakes has ended. Remedial work to prevent further discharges of dangerous pollutants is extremely expensive and time-consuming, however. It tends to lag unless public opinion remains strong and vocal. Government orders for improvement, enforced in some cases through court action, have been needed to make the laggards speed up their controls. The governments of the United States and Canada are working under a joint agreement for international cooperation against pollution of the lakes, a hopeful sign.

At the moment that progress began, at last, toward controlling discharges of wastes into the lakes, an angry dispute arose over an entirely new kind of potential damage to the water of the Great Lakes. This is called thermal pollution, a byproduct of a spectacular new use to which the Great Lakes will be put in the future.

12

Harnessing the Lakes

During the 350 years since Étienne Brûlé paddled out of the forest and saw Lake Huron rippling before him, the vessels borne on the waters of the Great Lakes have grown from birchbark canoes to mammoth diesel-powered ore carriers. The fur-trading posts have become cities of millions bound together by bands of concrete crowded with automobiles. The Indian tribes that fished in the lakes and trapped game on their shores have scattered, or their descendants live on out-of-the-way reservations given to them by the conquering white men. Instead of lying beyond the end of civilization, the chain of lakes is the water highway to mid-continent America. Pollution and the chopping up of their shores has damaged them, but they remain magnificent bodies of water. To astronauts orbiting the earth they look like a cluster of gleaming blue jewels.

Man's ingenuity never stands still. Two new forms of it are harnessing the Great Lakes to perform even greater service in the future for the 75 million people who live in the American and Canadian hinterlands that surround them. One is a spectacular feat of construction, the St. Lawrence Seaway. The other is nuclear power. The Great Lakes, and Lake Michigan in particular,

After the opening of the St. Lawrence Seaway in 1959, major Great Lakes ports became world ports.

are becoming a center for a heavy concentration of nuclear power plants.

Until recently, ships of large size and deep draft could move freely around the Great Lakes, but many of them could not sail out to the Atlantic Ocean because of the rapids and shoals in the St. Lawrence River between the eastern end of Lake Ontario and Montreal. Only small ones could fit through the old, narrow, shallow locks and canals that bypassed the obstacles in the river. Most of the cargo brought up the broad St. Lawrence from the rest of the world had to be unloaded at Montreal, then reloaded onto smaller vessels in order to reach Great Lakes ports. A few ships flying foreign flags sailed all the way to Chicago, but they were of shallow draft and limited capacity. The lakes were like a great city with wide boulevards and expressways within its city limits but connected to the outer world by a narrow two-lane road. What was needed was a liquid superhighway.

In a display of international cooperation, Canada and the United States in 1954 started construction of the St. Lawrence Seaway, the long-discussed project to provide the two countries with such a super-waterway. Their purpose was not only to provide a channel up the St. Lawrence River valley for deep draft ocean-going ships but to generate electrical power for the adjacent areas of both countries.

The problems faced by engineers in building this, the fourth-largest engineering project ever completed, were massive. At one time or another in the past, twenty-two small locks had been built around obstacles in the river beginning at the Lachine Rapids immediately above Montreal. These foamy, rocky rapids had been a barrier since the Indians portaged their canoes around them. Even for ships small enough to pass through the many locks, the time consumed in the process was uneconomical. In the Seaway, these twenty-two have been replaced by seven large locks, five built by Canada and two by the United States. These reduce passage time up the river and allow much larger ships to travel it.

At Montreal the river is only 20 feet above sea level; upstream at the junction with Lake Ontario, it is 235 feet. A vessel sailing

Locks of the St. Lawrence Seaway are operated around the clock. The St. Lambert Lock is the first of seven between Montreal and Lake Ontario.

up the Seaway is lifted 48 feet around the Lachine Rapids through the Canadian St. Lambert and Cote Ste. Catherine Locks; rises another 81 feet through the two Beauharnois Locks, also Canadian; 83 feet through the Snell and Eisenhower Locks, an American project; and the remaining three feet to Lake Ontario through the Iroquois Lock. Between the sets of locks, the vessel sails on lake-like sections of the river past farms on both sides. The international boundary runs down the middle of the stream part of the way. The ship passes through the dream-like Thousand Islands that stud the river—hundreds of tree-covered islands, some of them barely large enough to hold a house.

A small ocean ship enters the Upper Beauharnois Lock of the St. Lawrence Seaway, which lifts it forty-two feet on its voyage upstream to the Great Lakes.

These lake areas have been formed by river water trapped by dams, especially the Long Sault Spillway Dam and the Robert Moses—Robert H. Saunders Power Dam. Construction of these dams and the filling of Lake St. Lawrence behind them required removal of several hundred families from their farms and communities. Even cemeteries were moved to new locations. At the Eisenhower Lock a highway tunnel runs underneath the lock, so motorists have the unusual sensation of having a ship sail above their heads as they drive through.

Five years of work were required to build the Seaway. It was dedicated by President Dwight D. Eisenhower and Queen Elizabeth II in 1959. For administration purposes, the Welland Canal around Niagara Falls is considered part of the Seaway system. Depth of the waterway locks and canals is a uniform 27 feet. Since a ship must have clearance above the bottom, the actual maximum depth of ships in the water is 25.9 feet, sufficient for most of the ships that sail the oceans although too small for the gigantic

An Irish ship passes over the Eisenhower Tunnel as it enters the lock chamber at Eisenhower Lock on the St. Lawrence Seaway.

Aerial view of the flight locks of the Welland Canal near Thorold, Ontario

super-tankers of recent years. With the opening of the Seaway, cities around the Great Lakes all the way to Duluth at the far end of Lake Superior became seaports. It is commonplace to see the flags of more than thirty countries such as Norway, West Germany, Great Britain, Japan, Liberia, and France flapping at the stern of ships docked in lake harbors. The masters of the inbound ocean-going visitors must be careful not to overload their ships because they will sink deeper into the fresh water of the lakes than into salt water, one foot for every thirty-six feet of draft. The largest cargo hauled through the Seaway is iron ore from Labrador, carried upstream to the mills of Cleveland and other Lake Erie ports as a supplement to shipments from the Lake Superior mines.

Although the amount of ocean shipping to and from the Great Lakes increased spectacularly during the first decade of the Seaway's operation, the project was not the financial success it was expected to be. Costs of operation were so high that none of the nearly half billion dollars advanced by Canada and the United States to build the project could be repaid from the tolls collected.

One reason was the winter weather. Ice chokes the Seaway in December, so it must close down until early April. Crumpled blocks of drift ice pile up twenty feet high at some narrow points in the lakes. As many as forty in-bound ocean ships wait at Montreal for the ice-breakers to carve a path for them in the spring. Attempts are being made to lengthen the shipping season by such devices as heating the lock gates so they won't freeze and installing channel buoys of a type that won't be sliced off by ice.

While frozen water in the Great Lakes is a handicap for the Seaway, too much hot water in them became a center of controversy in their other new role, as the site of nuclear power plants.

The power for plants that generate electricity came traditionally from fossil fuels—coal, oil, and gas—or from water. Fossil fuels when burned produce heat energy which boils water into steam. The steam under pressure turns the blades of a shaft running through a generator. At the other end of the shaft is a magnet inside a coil of wire. As the magnet is revolved by the force of the

Ice halts much Great Lakes shipping in the winter.

steam striking the blades, electricity is produced. It is carried away from the generator by wires for distribution to homes, factories, and offices.

Generating plants powered by running water, called hydroelectric plants, operate on the same principle except that the energy to turn the blades of the turbine is provided by water funneled down at high speed from dammed-up ponds or from fast-moving rivers.

As the world's demand for electricity grew, so did the problem of producing enough of it. Fossil fuel plants have two important disadvantages—gradually they are exhausting the earth's stored-up supply of coal, oil, and gas, and the emissions from the plants burning these fossil fuels create air pollution. The number of hydroelectric plants is restricted because they must be located either at some natural source of fast-flowing water or at a man-created plant such as the St. Lawrence Seaway power complex where engineering can create a concentrated fall of water.

While far-seeing men were beginning to worry about the future supply of electricity, a marvelous new source of energy was discovered, nuclear power. This peacetime use of almost unlimited potential was a byproduct of development of the atomic bomb during World War II. Under pressure to find a super-weapon that the Allied Powers could use against their Axis enemies, scientists split the atom. This principle is called nuclear fission. It was used to arm the atomic bombs that United States planes dropped on Japanese cities in 1945, causing mass deaths of unprecedented numbers and forcing Japan to surrender.

From that moment, the world has lived under threat of "The Bomb." At the same time, it is benefiting from another application of the nuclear fission principle in the production of electric power.

Nuclear power plants are springing up across the United States at many places. In the early 1980's they should be producing more than 10 per cent of the country's electricity. The Great Lakes have become the site of many nuclear plants, because the plants require a large supply of water and the millions of persons living near the lakes seem insatiable in their need for more electricity. Lake Michigan is being circled with nuclear plants. In the early 1970's a dozen such plants were either in operation or being de-

Big Rock Point nuclear power plant on Lake Michigan near Charlevoix, Michigan

Palisades nuclear plant, with capacity of 800,000 kilowatts, during final stages of construction near South Haven, Michigan.

veloped around the lakes, seven of them on Lake Michigan.

In a nuclear power plant, the heat produced by splitting the atom is used to boil water into steam that turns the turbine shaft. From there on, the process is similar to that in fossil-fueled and hydroelectric plants. This is how that heat is created: When an atom of uranium fuel stored in the power plant reactor is struck by a particle called a neutron, it splits into two parts. This is fission. Each of these parts becomes an atom. However, the weight of the two new atoms combined is slightly less than their parent atom's. The residue becomes heat-producing energy. The action of splitting an atom releases two or three neutrons; these particles strike and split other atoms, creating a chain reaction. The millions of splitting actions continue as long as the reactor is turned on, thus creating a constant flow of heating for warming the water. The heat created by splitting an individual atom is infinitesimal. To produce one kilowatt of heat requires thirty trillion fissions per second.

The pace of the atom splitting inside the reactor is controlled by a series of rods containing a neutron-absorbing material such as boron or cadmium. The farther out these rods are pulled, reducing the amount of neutron-blocking material in the reactor, the greater the amount of fission. In reverse, when the control rods are pushed in all the way the chain reaction is broken and the reactor stops operating. The uranium fuel in the reactor is in small pellet form contained within rods of zirconium alloy. These can be removed and replaced as the uranium pellets gradually lose their strength.

Scientists and engineers are developing an even more advanced type of nuclear power generation called a fast-breeder reactor. In this, more fuel is created by the fission process than is actually burned; this can be used to replenish the reactor. Since liquid sodium is used as a coolant, the problem of thermal pollution disappears. Construction of large, efficient, commercial-sized fast breeder reactors lies in the future, however.

Since the atom-splitting process involves potentially fatal radioactivity, extreme precautions are necessary to shield it and prevent human exposure. Because of these precautions, the risk to people living or working near a nuclear plant is considered negligible. The reactor is of tightly sealed metal encased in concrete. Water circulating through the closed circuit of a pressurized-water reactor is heated by the fission to approximately 600 degrees Fahrenheit. Passing through the pipes of a boiler, it heats an enclosed secondary supply of water that circulates outside these pipes to approximately 500 degrees. The primary water supply never leaves the reactor or touches the water in the secondary system, which becomes steam and turns the turbines. A third water circuit, the only one that reaches the outside world, then goes to work. The water in the secondary circuit must be cooled from steam back to liquid form before it is recirculated to take on a new heat charge and become steam again. This is accomplished by circulating around the outside of the secondary pipes a flow of water at ordinary temperature, which is pumped in from a nearby stream or lake. While reducing the temperature of the secondary circuit water, which it never touches, the cooling circuit water

Ocean vessels and pleasure craft share the channel of the St. Lawrence Seaway at Brockville, Ontario.

absorbs heat. This water is then pumped back into the body of water from which it was drawn.

That is the point at which a quarrel arises between the power companies and the campaigners to protect our natural environment. The water that flows back into Lake Michigan from the nuclear plants is many degrees warmer than it was when drawn from the lake, as much as 21 degrees warmer at one large plant. Environmentalists claim that the heavy flow of heated water into the lake from several nuclear plants, day and night, year after year, will upset the living conditions of plant and fish life. They call the change thermal pollution. In their view, after a few years the natural balance of life in the lake might be dangerously upset by a rise in the lake-water temperature. Cold water fish in particular might be affected.

"Not so," say the power companies and the scientists who agree with them. "The hot water cools so rapidly in a plume at the discharge point well offshore that it can do no harm in such a huge lake."

"Why take a chance of ruining our natural heritage?" the conservation groups reply.

The problem can be solved by construction of cooling towers at each nuclear plant, down which the water tumbles to be cooled off by the air. Since these towers are expensive to build and operate, the power companies have tried to avoid constructing them. Some companies agreed to build towers when conservation groups and the federal Environmental Protection Agency applied heavy public pressure. Others fought in court to avoid having to do so.

Unfortunately it is an argument to which nobody has a positive answer yet. There can be none until a flow of warm water has gone into the lake for several years, long enough to show whether the environment really is changed. But if it is changed, can the damage be undone?

So the Great Lakes, born from the icy waters of the retreating glaciers, have become a testing ground in man's dilemma of providing for the physical needs of a growing population without destroying the natural resources of the earth that we humans inherited in such abundance and must preserve for our descendants.

Bibliography

Among the many publications concerning the Great Lakes, the following were especially helpful in the preparation of this book:

BLAIR, EMMA HELEN, ed. *Indian Tribes of the Upper Mississippi Valley*, especially the section "Memoir on the Manners, Customs and Religion of the Savages of North America," by Nicholas Perrot. Cleveland: Clark, 1911

BOWEN, DANA THOMAS. *Lore of the Lakes.* Daytona Beach, Fla.: Bowen, 1940

BOWEN, DANA THOMAS. *Memories of the Lakes.* Daytona Beach, Fla.: Bowen, 1946

CHAMPLAIN, SAMUEL DE. *Voyages 1604–18.* New York: Charles Scribner's Sons, 1907

CONDON, GEORGE E. *Cleveland, the Best Kept Secret.* New York: Doubleday and Co., Inc., 1967

DUTTON, CHARLES J. *Oliver Hazard Perry.* New York: Longmans, Green and Co., 1935

GRAHAM, LLOYD. *Niagara Country.* New York: Duell, Sloan and Pearce, 1949

HATCHER, HARLAN. *The Great Lakes.* New York: Oxford University Press, 1944

HATCHER, HARLAN and WALTER, ERICH A. *A Pictorial History of the Great Lakes.* New York: Crown Publishers, 1963

HAVIGHURST, WALTER. *The Great Lakes Reader*. New York: The Macmillan Co., 1966

HAVIGHURST, WALTER. *The Long Ships Passing*. New York: The Macmillan Co., 1942

HAVIGHURST, WALTER. *Three Flags at the Straits*. Englewood Cliffs, N.J.: Prentice-Hall, 1966

HENRY, ALEXANDER. *Travels and Adventures in Canada and Indian Territories*. Boston: Little, Brown and Co., 1901

HUBBS, CARL L. and LAGLER, KARL F. *Fishes of the Great Lakes Region*. Ann Arbor: University of Michigan Press, 1958

JENNINGS, JESSE D. *Prehistory of North America*. New York: McGraw-Hill Book Co., Inc., 1968.

KINIETZ, W. VERNON. *The Indians of the Upper Great Lakes 1616–1760*, especially the section "Memoir Concerning the Different Indian Nations of North America," by Antoine Denis Raudot. Ann Arbor: University of Michigan Press, 1965

MALKUS, ALIDA. *Blue-Water Boundary*. New York: Hastings House, 1960

MAYER, HAROLD M. and WADE, RICHARD C. *Chicago, Growth of a Metropolis*. Chicago: University of Chicago Press, 1969

McKEE, RUSSELL. *Great Lakes Country*. New York: Thomas Y. Crowell Co., 1966

MICHIGAN WATER RESOURCES COMMISSION. *Michigan and the Great Lakes*. Lansing: 1967

QUIMBY, GEORGE IRVING. *Indian Life in the Upper Great Lakes, 11,000 B.C. to 1800 A.D.* Chicago: University of Chicago Press, 1960

THWAITES, REUBEN GOLD, ed. *Jesuit Relations and Allied Documents*. Cleveland: Burrows, 1900

Index

About the Author

Phil Ault, associate editor of the *South Bend Tribune*, is a veteran newspaper editor in the United States and abroad. During World War II he was a war correspondent in North Africa and Iceland, and chief of the London bureau of United Press.

A native of Illinois, he grew up near the Great Lakes and, since returning to the Midwest after twenty years in California, he has traveled extensively around the lakes.

He lives on the St. Joseph River near the place where La Salle made an important portage during his exploration of the lakes three hundred years ago.

This is Ault's ninth book, including college textbooks. Among those he has written for young adults is the prize-winning *This Is the Desert*, an anecdotal history of the Southwest desert. His most recent book for children is *Wonders of the Mosquito World*.